books designed with giving in mind

Crepes & Omelets
Microwave Cooking
Vegetable Cookbook
Kid's Arts and Crafts
Bread Baking
The Crockery Pot Cookbook
Kid's Garden Book
Classic Greek Cooking
The Compleat American
   Housewife 1776
Low Carbohydrate Cookbook

Kid's Cookbook
Italian
Cheese Guide & Cookbook
Miller's German
Quiche & Souffle
To My Daughter, With Love
Natural Foods
Chinese Vegetarian
Jewish Gourmet
Working Couples

Mexican
Sunday Breakfast
Fisherman's Wharf Cookbook
Ice Cream Cookbook
Hippo Hamburger
Blender Cookbook
The Wok, a Chinese Cookbook
Cast Iron Cookbook
Japanese Country
Fondue Cookbook

from nitty gritty productions

To Yves Gaétan

May your day be like milk.
                    —a Bedouin toast

The CHEESE
Guide & Cookbook

Featuring recipes from the world's great cuisines and a glossary of cheeses and cheese terms.

BY ANN CHANDONNET

Illustrated by CRAIG TORLUCCI

A Nitty Gritty Book*
Published by
Nitty Gritty Productions
P. O. Box 5457
Concord, California 94524

*Nitty Gritty Books - Trademark
Owned by Nitty Gritty Productions
Concord, California

ISBN 0-911954-26-0

Contents

Introduction

Man has at one time or another consumed milk from the cow, goat, sheep, buffalo, yak, zebu, mare, ass, camel, sow, llama, reindeer, and whale. The prehistoric Swiss lake dwellers (4000-2000 BC) tamed bovines and from their milk made butter and cheese. Freizes from a temple at Ur of the Chaldees show milking scenes of 4000 BC, and a Babylonian medical text of the same antiquity expresses the hope that a sick man may be made "as pure as yogurt." The ancient Egyptians often pictured the heavens as a cow with a full udder—perhaps the original of the cow that jumped over the moon?

H. G. Wells once wrote that civilization began when huntsmen turned herdsmen. When herdsmen turned dairymen, the ancient Greeks claimed that such a delicacy as cheese must have been invented by the gods. The Romans and Hebrews used cheese as an army ration. David was taking cheese to the Israelites when he met Goliath.

Cheese was originally made to use up surplus milk. For pre-refrigeration man, the virtue of cheese was that it kept longer than milk. In many countries, where meat is less plentiful and more dear than in the U.S., cheese is often used in its place to furnish the bulk of the diet's protein.

The creation of cheese involves a number of chemical processes. Simply put, milk is coagulated by the addition of some form of rennet. (Rennet contains an enzyme which occurs in the gastric juices of calves.) This causes the curd to separate from the whey. The curd is cut into pieces and then pressed into shape in a hoop or mold, cured, and aged. Cheeses may be (1) fresh—that is, unfermented curds (such as cream cheese, ricotta, Neufchatel) or (2) fermented, the latter divided further into soft (Brie, Stilton, Camembert) and hard (Cheddar, Edam, Emmenthal, American, Munster, Monterey Jack).

In 1972 Americans consumed 2 1/2 billion pounds of cheese, including 136 million pounds of imported cheese (twice as much as in 1961). Brie, Camembert, Emmenthal, Gruyere, Edam, and Gouda were prominent among the imports. But if you travel a great deal abroad, you are aware that imported cheeses do not taste the same as cheeses consumed on their home soil. The difference is the result of federal law that requires that either pasteurized milk be used in cheese, or that the cheese be aged for at least 60 days, before export is permitted to this country—because of the possibility of undulant germs in raw milk. Abroad, you eat cheeses made of raw milk, and with, perhaps, a more pronounced flavor. This accounts for the difference between Parmesan which was made in the U. S., and Italian Parmesan.

Cheese is a very high protein food, ranging from 12 grams of protein per ounce (Parmesan) to 6 grams (Blue). Domestic or imported, cheese is big business. Per capita consumption has risen over 40% in the last decade. We hope the information in this guide will help you become more knowledgeable and adventurous in your personal cheese choices and the following recipes will encourage you to add more of this delicious food from the gods to your daily diet.

Appetizers & Dips

With its wide range of flavors, cheese can add a great deal of variety to our menus. The Greek comic poet Antiphanes included it in his list of seasonings in the company of salt, thyme, sesame, honey, onions, mustard, lime, parsley, and green fig juice. In Greece today, any visitor will be greeted with appetizers-- cucumbers, white goat's cheese, homemade bread, olives, or hot cheese pastries.

Try to serve at least two appetizers, preferably one hot and one cold. If you are short of time, simple cubes of different cheeses served with toothpicks will serve to whet the appetite for the meal to come.

CHEESE & ARTICHOKE TARTS

This is a flavorful hot appetizer with a surprise center—a tender artichoke heart.

4 baked patty shells (homemade or frozen) about 3 x 1 1/4 inches
6 oz. cream cheese with chives, softened at room temperature
2 T soft butter
1 large egg
3 drops tabasco sauce
6 drops Worcestershire sauce
4 artichoke hearts (canned, or frozen—cooked)

Place patty shells on a bakeproof serving dish. Beat the cream cheese with the egg and the seasonings.

Just before baking, place a spoonful of cheese in each shell, set an artichoke heart in the center, and cover with remaining cheese. Bake for about 30 minutes in the upper third of a 475° oven, or until cheese filling has puffed slightly and browned on top. Serve immediately. Four appetizers.

OLIVE ANCHOVY CANAPÉS

12 large pitted green olives, finely chopped
2 oz. can of anchovy fillets, drained
2 hard-boiled eggs, finely chopped
3 oz. cream cheese, at room temperature
1/2 cup chopped walnuts
1/4 cup finely chopped parsley, paprika, or black olives

Mash together the green olives, anchovy fillets and cream cheese. Blend in the hard-boiled eggs and walnuts.

Divide mixture evenly into 24 pieces. Shape into balls and roll in parsley, paprika, or olives. Chill thoroughly before serving.

VARIATION: Replace anchovies with 4 oz. liverwurst for Olive Liverwurst Canapés; omit walnuts or replace with 1/4 cup chopped water chestnuts. Makes 24 canapes.

EGGS STUFFED WITH RICOTTA

1 dozen large eggs, hard-boiled
1 cup ricotta cheese
seasoned salt of your choice, to taste
pepper
2 T finely minced green onion
1/2 t dry mustard
parsley and slivers of pimiento or pickled red pepper to garnish

Shell eggs carefully and split lengthwise. Scoop out yolks and mash with a fork. Mix with cheese and seasonings. Taste to make certain seasoning is correct; add a little garlic powder at this point if you wish. Fill whites with mixture and refrigerate, lightly covered, until serving time; may be prepared 1 day in advance. Garnish each half with a sprig of parsley and a sliver of pimiento or red pepper; or make an X on each half with pimiento, and garnish with parsley. Makes 24 halves.

HAM MUSHROOM PUFFS

2 1/4 oz. can deviled ham
24 circles of bread, 1 1/2'' in diameter
24 fresh mushrooms, with caps no larger in diameter than bread circles
2 T bacon drippings
3 oz. cream cheese, at room temperature
1 egg yolk
dash onion powder or garlic powder

Toast bread circles on one side in oven broiler; don't dry out excessively.

Cut stems from mushrooms and saute caps gently in bacon drippings until tender. (Keep stems for another dish.)

12

Beat together deviled ham, cream cheese, egg yolk, and onion (or garlic) powder until light and blended. Arrange a mushroom cap on each bread circle, rounded side up. Place a spoonful of the ham mixture over each, covering completely—as if putting meringue on a pie. Place in a 350° oven for 5 to 7 minutes, or until lightly browned. Serve at once.

NOTE: If you want to prepare these ahead, after topping with ham mixture, cover and refrigerate. Makes 24 canapes.

OLIVES IN PASTRY

1 cup sharp cheddar cheese, grated
1/4 cup butter or margarine, at room temperature
3/4 cup flour
8 oz. pimiento-stuffed olives, or pitted, ripe olives stuffed with almond slivers:
    about 36
sesame or poppy seed, or paprika

Blend cheese with butter. Stir in flour and knead briefly to form a dough. Drain olives on paper towels to absorb liquid. Wrap dough (about 1 t) around each olive so the olive is covered completely. Coat with sesame seed, poppy seed, or paprika.

At this point the pastry-covered olives may be chilled or frozen. Thaw before baking.

Place on ungreased baking sheet and bake 15 minutes at 400° or until baked but not browned. Serve warm. (May be baked just slightly ahead and reheated for serving.) 3 dozen canapés. Makes three dozen canapes.

PORTED CHEESE

1 cup finely grated cheddar (or cheddar cheese spread)
1/4 cup crumbled blue cheese
3 to 4 T Tinta Cream Port

   Beat together until blended. Cover and refrigerate several hours or longer to mellow flavors. Remove from refrigerator 1 hour before serving. Serve with apple pie or fresh fruit as a dessert or with crackers to accompany cocktails. Makes about 1 1/4 cups.

DEVILED CHEESE ASPIC

This jellied appetizer spread is very unusual and may be prepared 24 hours in advance of your dinner or party.

1 t unflavored gelatin
1 cup consomme
4 1/2 oz. deviled ham
3 oz. cream cheese, softened at room temperature
melba toast or crackers

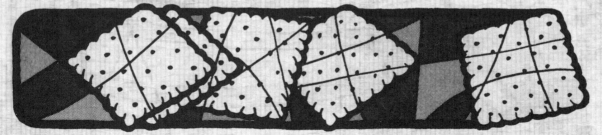

Add gelatin to cold consomme and let soften for 5 minutes. Heat, stirring constantly, until gelatin is dissolved. Pour 1/3 cup into a 5 x 2 x 2 1/2 inch loaf pan or other mold. Chill until set. Keep remaining consomme warm so that it doesn't gel.

When first layer is set, mix deviled ham with cream cheese until fluffy. Spoon into mold on top of firm consomme and spread into an even layer. Pour remaining liquid consomme over top. Chill for several hours or overnight. Unmold and serve with knives for spreading and toast or crackers. Makes 6 servings.

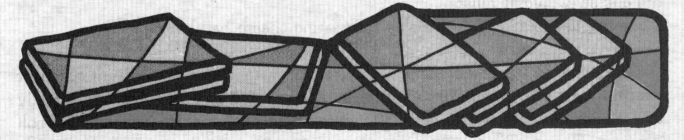

CORNED BEEF & CHEESE BALL

8 oz. cream cheese, softened at room temperature
2 cups grated cheddar cheese
12 oz. can of corned beef, shredded
2 t horseradish
1 1/2 t prepared mustard
1/2 t Worcestershire sauce
1/2 t freshly grated lemon peel
3 T fresh lemon juice
3/4 cup sweet pickle relish
1 cup snipped (finely) fresh parsley for coating cheese ball before serving.

Combine all ingredients thoroughly, either with mixer at medium speed or hands. Shape into a ball. Wrap tightly in plastic or foil and refrigerate until ready to use. Remove from refrigerator 30 minutes before serving. Reshape ball and roll in finely snipped parsley until completely covered. Serve with assorted crackers, pretzels, orange sections, and/or other fresh fruits.

VARIATION: Substitute 1/2 cup finely chopped dried beef for the corned beef and omit the pickle relish. Make into a log, 1 or 2 inches in diameter. Wrap in foil and refrigerate until ready to serve. Thirty minutes before serving, remove Dried Beef-Cheese Log from refrigerator. Sprinkle a sheet of waxed paper with paprika, and roll the log on it to coat. Serve in slices on crackers or melba toast rounds. One 5 to 6-inch ball.

APPETIZER CHEESE CAKE

This appetizer "cake" is especially good with d'Anjou, Bosc, or Comice pears. Be sure to buy the pears a few days ahead so they will be fully ripe.

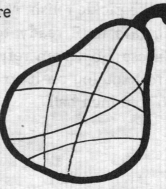

1 box (6 oz.) cheese crackers, finely crushed
8 oz. cream cheese, softened at room temperature
1 cup sour cream
1/2 cup finely chopped, stuffed green olives
1/2 cup finely chopped celery
1/2 cup finely chopped green pepper
1/4 cup finely chopped onion
2 T lemon juice
1 t Worcestershire sauce
1 t salt

4 drops tabasco sauce
stuffed green olives for garnish, and 1 pear per person

Beat cream cheese until smooth. Blend in sour cream, chopped olives, celery, green pepper, onion, lemon juice, Worcestershire, salt, and tabasco.

Oil a 7-inch or 9-inch spring form pan. Cover the bottom with half the crushed cheese crackers. Spread cheese mixture over cracker base and sprinkle remaining crumbs evenly over top of "cake."

Cover, or slide cake into a large plastic bag, and refrigerate overnight. Garnish with a border of sliced stuffed green olives.

To serve, remove sides of pan and cut cake into wedges. Serve with pear wedges. Guests should be supplied with fruit knives and small plates. Serves 8 to 10.

HERBED CHEESE CROCK

Certainly you've seen those crocks of cheese for sale. If you have an empty crock around the kitchen, fill it with your own creation.

10 oz. Muenster cheese
1/2 lb. aged cheddar cheese
3 T brandy
1/8 t sweet basil, crushed

1/16 t dried dill weed
1 t Dijon mustard
1/2 t paprika
2 T softened butter

Grate the cheeses. Put into a mixing bowl with remaining ingredients. Beat until well blended. Cover and refrigerate until an hour before serving, then remove so that the mixture will reach room temperature and flavors will be at their best. Makes 3 cups.

VARIATION: Use only cheddar cheese.

CHEDDAR-COTTAGE DIP

2 cups cottage cheese
2 t grated onion
1 t celery salt
1/4 t Worcestershire sauce
2 cups (8 oz.) shredded cheddar cheese

In a small mixing bowl beat together cottage cheese, onion, celery salt, and Worcestershire sauce at highest speed of mixer (or by hand) until smooth. Gradually add half the cheddar and continue beating until smooth. Then fold in other half of cheddar. Makes approximately 3 cups.

INDIAN SPREAD

8 oz. cream cheese, softened at room temperature
1 cup shredded sharp cheddar cheese
2 T sherry or lemon juice
1/2 t curry powder
1/4 t salt
1/4 cup chopped chutney
1 T chopped fresh chives

    Mix cream cheese, cheddar cheese, sherry, curry powder, salt, and chutney together until smooth. Put into a dip dish and sprinkle with chives. Serve with crackers. (Note: One curried dish in a menu is usually enough for American palates, so make the main dish un-curried.) Makes about 2 cups.

    VARIATION: Replace cheddar cheese with 1/2 cup dairy sour cream. Serve with seafood or fruit. Makes about 2 cups of spread

ANCHOVY DIP

1 1/2 cups cottage cheese
5 drained anchovy filets, finely chopped
2 t grated onion
1/2 cup sour cream
1/4 cup finely chopped green pepper or parsley
1 T chopped pimiento

Beat together in a small bowl the cottage cheese, anchovies, and onion; when fairly smooth, stir in green pepper and pimiento. About 2 cups.

VARIATION: For Sardine Dip, replace anchovies with 1 can (4 3/8 oz.) skinless and boneless sardines in oil, drained.

Serve Anchovy Dip with crackers, potato chips, pretzels, or fresh raw vegetables: cucumber, celery and carrot sticks, radish roses, tomato wedges, cauliflowerets, green onions, etc.

BLUE-MUSTARD DIP

2 cups grated cheddar cheese
2 T blue or Roquefort cheese
1/4 cup mayonnaise
2 T prepared mustard
2 t horseradish
3 to 4 T milk

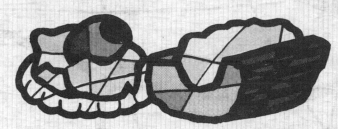

Blend cheeses until smooth. Add remaining ingredients, except milk, and mix well. Beat in enough milk to make a good dipping consistency. (If you get it too thin, add more grated cheddar.) Serve with potato chips, corn chips, pretzels, breadsticks, or crackers (non-cheese flavored). About 1 1/2 cups.

Other ideas: Use to stuff celery stalks or hollowed-out tomatoes. In the latter case, mix a little of the tomato pulp with the dip.

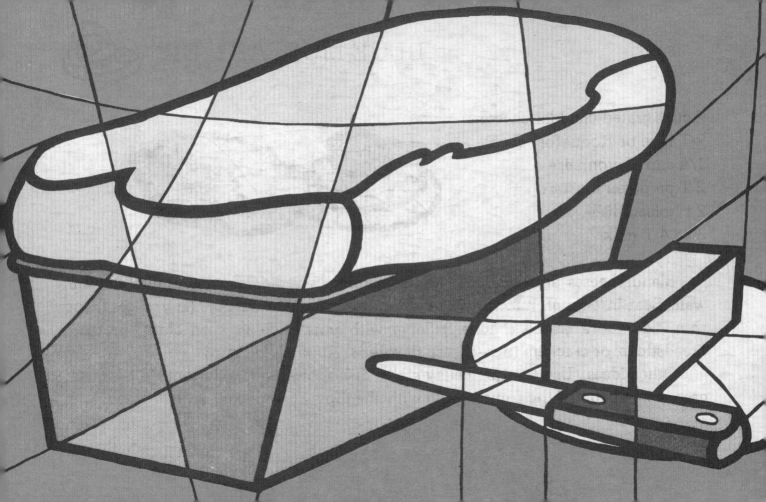

Breads & Breakfast Dishes

In Turkey, natives of Istanbul begin the day with white cheese, olives, honey, and brown bread. Israelis breakfast on fresh cottage cheese, yogurt, bread, oranges. Consider following suit for a nutritious, tasty change of pace. If you balk at olives, substitute bananas or prunes. Try brown sugar on plain yogurt—a favorite in our home—with peaches or other fruit in season and warm cheese bread.

31

CHEESE BREAD

This bread is especially good served with hot broth and plenty of butter. To keep, seal tightly in a plastic bag and refrigerate.

2 cups hot water
3 T sugar
3 T vegetable shortening or butter
2 1/2 t salt
2 cups nonfat dry milk

1 pkg. active dry yeast
1/2 lb. sharp cheddar cheese, shredded
5 cups flour
1 T vegetable shortening, melted

Put hot water in a large mixing bowl. Add sugar, butter, salt, and stir until shortening is melted. Cool to lukewarm.

When lukewarm, sprinkle yeast on top and stir. Let stand 5 minutes to activate, then stir in dry milk and cheese.

Add 3 cups of flour to cheese mixture. Beat until batter is smooth and will fall from your spoon in sheets. Add remaining flour. Stir until dough forms a ball and comes away from sides of bowl easily. Turn dough onto lightly floured board.

Knead until smooth and elastic—about 10 minutes. Place ball of dough in a large greased bowl. Brush top of dough with melted shortening. Cover with clean, damp towel and set in warm place (80° to 85°) to rise, free from drafts. Let rise until double in bulk; this will take about 2 hours. Punch down dough. Cover with towel and let rise again until almost double—about 1 hour.

Remove dough from bowl and return to board. Shape into smooth round ball. Cut in half with sharp knife. Shape each half into a smooth round ball, cover and let rest 10 minutes. Then mold each ball to fit greased loaf pan 9 x 5 x 3" or casserole of your choice. Place in pans. Cover with towel. Let rise 45 minutes.

Bake at 350° for 40 minutes, or until crust is an even brown color and makes a hollow sound when tapped. Remove bread from pans. Cool on wire rack. Makes 2 loaves.

QUICK CHEESE BREAD

This is a quick (non-yeast) bread, which tastes better and slices more easily if cooled and "aged" overnight.

1 cup milk
2 1/3 cups sifted flour
3/4 cup sugar
4 t baking powder
1/4 t baking soda
1 t salt
1 cup coarsely shredded cheddar cheese
1 egg, slightly beaten
1 T melted butter

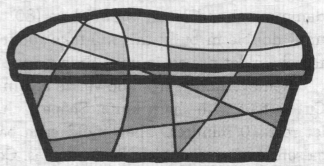

Sift together flour, sugar, baking powder, baking soda, and salt. Mix in cheese.

Make a well in the center of these dry ingredients.

Beat egg with melted butter, and then combine with milk. Pour egg mixture into well, and stir in dry ingredients until all are moistened. Pour into a greased 8 1/2 x 4 1/2 x 2 1/2 inch loaf pan. Bake at 325° for 55 to 60 minutes, or until bread tests done with a cake tester inserted in center. Remove loaf from oven and cool in the pan on a wire rack for 10 minutes. Then remove loaf from pan and complete cooling.

When loaf is cool, wrap tightly and store overnight before slicing. This bread is also good toasted. Makes 1 loaf.

VARIATION: Scald milk. Pour over 1 cup chopped, pitted dates, or 1 cup dried currants and let stand 5 minutes before mixing with egg and melted butter. Makes 1 loaf.

CHEESE BUTTERMILK BISCUITS

2 cups flour
2 t baking powder
1/4 t baking soda
1 t salt
1/2 t oregano, or rosemary, or dill weed
1/3 cup grated Parmesan or Parmesan-Romano blend
1/4 cup shortening
3/4 cup buttermilk
1 T melted butter

Sift together flour, baking powder, baking soda, salt, and oregano. Mix in cheese, then cut in shortening finely. Stir in buttermilk. Turn dough out on well-floured board, and knead lightly. Divide into 12 equal pieces and roll each into a ball with a floured hand.

Space each ball evenly in a well-greased 9-inch round layer cake pan. Brush tops with melted butter and sprinkle with a little more cheese, if desired.

Biscuits may be made ahead, covered, and refrigerated for up to 4 hours before baking. Bake at 425° for 20 minutes, or until browned. Makes 1 dozen biscuits.

VARIATION: Use fresh milk instead of buttermilk; use 2 1/2 t baking powder, and omit baking soda.

Dill is good with fish; oregano, with beef; and rosemary, with chicken.

SWISS CHEESE BREAD

If you are a fan of unsliced white bread (enriched, salt-rising, sourdough, or French), you may like to slice it, adorn it, and heat it to serve with other foods. Both of the following could complete a meal when served with a hearty vegetable soup. The garlic version is also delicious with steak.

1 loaf unsliced white bread
1 pkg. (6 oz.) Swiss cheese slices
1/2 cup butter or margarine
1/3 cup instant minced onion flakes
3 T prepared mustard
1 T poppy seeds (optional)
2 t lemon juice
2 bacon slices

Cut bread in 3/4" thick slices, almost through the bottom crust. (Cut all the way through if your guests don't like to fight the crust as they pluck a slice.)

Cream together the butter, onion, mustard, poppy seed, lemon juice, and spread on bread slices. Insert 1 slice cheese in each cut; press back into loaf shape. Place in greased 9-inch baking dish. Cut bacon slices in half and arrange four pieces over top—parallel or in two x's. Bake at 350° for 20 minutes or until bacon has cooked and cheese is melted. Serves 4 to 6.

GARLIC FRENCH BREAD / PARMESAN

1 loaf French bread
1/2 cup soft butter or margarine
3 T grated Parmesan cheese
1 t dried majoram leaves, crushed
1 clove garlic, mashed or crushed
1/4 t pepper
dash cayenne (optional)

Slice bread, not to bottom crust, but almost. Combine butter with rest of ingredients. Place bread on a cookie sheet or in a baking dish. Spread butter mixture between slices. Sprinkle top of loaf lightly with a few drops cold water; bake at 350° for 10 minutes. Serve at once. (This should be done at the last minute or bread will dry out; if you prepare ahead or if your guests are late, wrap in foil before heating.) Serves 4 to 6.

CHEESE COFFEE RINGS

This is the delicious "Cheese Danish" in ring form. Delicious for breakfast, tea, or snacks, and almost as rich as cheesecake.

1/3 cup sugar
1 t salt
1 pkg. plus 1 t active dry yeast
about 4 cups flour
1/4 cup butter or margarine

1 cup milk
2 whole eggs and 2 egg yolks
Cheese Filling (page 44)
1 1/2 cups raisins or currants
Frosting (page 44)

Mix sugar, salt, yeast, and 1 1/4 cups flour in large bowl of an electric mixer.

Put butter and milk in a small saucepan and heat until butter is melted. Gradually add to dry ingredients and beat at medium speed for 2 minutes, scraping bowl occasionally. Add whole eggs and 1 egg yolk and 3/4 cup more flour. Beat at high speed, scraping sides of bowl, 2 more minutes. With wooden spoon, stir in enough additional flour to make a soft dough. Place in a greased bowl, cover with plastic wrap and chill at least 2 hours.

After chilling, divide the dough in half. Then roll out each half on lightly floured board to form a 16 x 10" rectangle. Spread each rectangle with half the filling, sprinkle with half the raisins, and roll up, starting from long side. Seal long edge. Arrange, sealed edge down, in a circle on greased baking sheet, and seal ends to form a ring. At 1 1/2 inch intervals, snip two-thirds of way into the ring with kitchen shears, and turn each section on its side. Brush with remaining egg yolk, beaten with 1 t cold water.

Let rise, uncovered, in warm place 1 hour, or until light. Bake at 375° for about 20 minutes. While still warm, brush with frosting. Cool on racks before cutting. Refrigerate leftovers because of dairy content. Makes 2 rings.

Cheese Filling:

11 oz. cream cheese, softened at room temperature
8 oz. creamed small curd cottage cheese
1 t vanilla extract
1/2 cup sugar
2 egg yolks
1/2 t cinnamon

Beat all ingredients together until blended.

Frosting:

This is actually a glaze and may be used on any buns or coffee cakes. Mix 1 1/2 cup confectioners' sugar with 2 T milk or cream or warm water and 1/2 t vanilla or almond extract.

BAKED EGGS WITH CHEDDAR

These are good for a hearty breakfast, a light lunch, or late supper.

4 slices fresh bread
1/4 cup melted butter or margarine
1/2 cup shredded sharp or mild cheddar cheese
1/2 to 1 t thyme

4 eggs
1/3 cup light cream or milk
1/2 t salt

Crumble the bread (which may be white, whole wheat, or rye—depending on your preference) and place in a shallow pie plate or casserole. (Or this may be made in four individual ramekins.) Pour melted butter over crumbs. Bake at 350° for 15 minutes to brown lightly. Remove from oven. Sprinkle shredded cheese over top. Break eggs onto the cheese. Combine the cream, thyme, and salt; heat gently and pour over the eggs. Bake at 350° for 15 more minutes or until eggs are set. (The yolks will set before the whites do.) Serve at once. 4 servings, 1 egg each or 2 servings, 2 eggs each.

MEXICAN CORN BREAD

This is a double corn bread, with both kernels and corn meal. Delicious with chili.

1 can (8 1/2 oz.) cream-style corn
1 cup yellow corn meal
2 eggs
1 t salt
1/2 t soda
3/4 cup milk
1/3 cup melted lard, butter or margarine
1/2 cup grated sharp cheddar cheese
1 can (4 oz.) mild diced chilies (Optional)
2 T butter

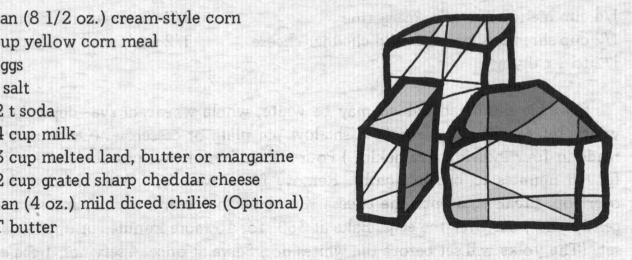

46

Combine the cream-style corn, corn meal, eggs, salt, soda, milk, lard, half the cheese, and all the chilies. Beat well.

Meanwhile, in a 400° oven, put the two T of butter in a 1 1/2 quart casserole (the heavier the better) or a nine-inch ovenproof skillet. Leave in oven until butter is melted but not browned.

Immediately pour in the corn bread batter. Sprinkle the top with the remaining cheese and bake 40 minutes or until it tests done in the center. Serve warm. Serves 8.

CHEESE POPOVERS

Serve these popovers with grapefruit halves, eggs or sausage, and plenty of butter—and listen to the music of compliments for your culinary skill.

2 eggs
1 cup milk
1 cup flour
1/2 t salt
1/3 cup finely grated cheddar

Beat eggs and milk together until blended thoroughly. Add flour, salt, cheese, and beat just until smooth. Pour into 9 well-buttered muffin tins, or custard cups, or popover wells, and bake at 425° for 45 minutes. Serve at once.

May be cooled, frozen and reheated, or split, and served with creamed fish or eggs for dinner. Makes 9 popovers.

SUNDAY MORNING SCRAMBLED EGGS

If, like so many of us, you are in the habit of having a late breakfast on weekends, try this egg recipe next weekend. (The following weekend you can try Cottage Crescents.)

6 eggs	1/2 cup creamed cottage cheese	1/8 t pepper
1/2 t salt	1/4 cup milk	2 T butter
1/2 t whole dried rosemary		

In a medium size bowl beat together lightly the eggs, salt, rosemary, milk, and pepper.

In a medium skillet, melt the butter. When hot, pour in egg mixture and reduce heat. Cook slowly, gently lifting from bottom and sides with a spoon or spatula as mixture begins to set. Then fold in cottage cheese and continue cooking until eggs reach desired degree of firmness. Makes 4 servings.

 # COTTAGE CRESCENTS

8 oz. creamed cottage cheese
1 cup butter or margarine
2 cups flour
3/4 cup light brown sugar
1/4 cup butter or margarine
2 T water
3/4 cup finely chopped walnuts
dash of cinnamon
1 egg yolk

In a bowl, blend with pastry fork or blender the cottage cheese and the cup of butter. Then blend in the flour until the dough forms a smooth ball.

Combine brown sugar, cinnamon, and walnuts in a bowl. Melt the remaining 1/4 cup of butter.

On lightly floured board, roll 1/3 of the dough into a circle, 1/8 inch thick. Brush with 1/3 of the melted butter; sprinkle with 1/3 of the nut mixture. Cut circle into 16 wedges. Beginning at outer (wide) end, roll up each wedge tightly and place, point-side down, on a greased cookie sheet. (You will need three greased cookie sheets unless you rotate.)

Beat egg yolk with water, and brush on tops of crescents. Bake about 20 minutes at 400° or until golden. Repeat with remaining dough. Makes 4 dozen crescents.

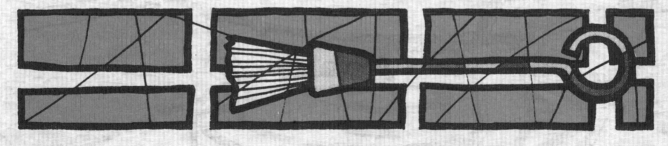

Finger Foods

Forks were introduced into Italy by the Byzantines in the eleventh century, did not reach England until the fourteenth, and were not really in general use until the seventeenth. Before this, men might occasionally hack at a tough bit with a knife, but generally they picked up their food and chomped and gnawed quite freely. Thus modern man's seemingly atavistic predilection for finger foods does not hark back to so remote an ancestor as he might fear (or hope)! As any child can tell you, there is nothing more natural, and more fun, than picking up your food. If you can scoop up poi, why not a piragie?

53

CHEESE FONDUE

Cheese fondue requires a few special utensils: a fondue pot (earthenware is traditional for cheese) and a long-handled fondue fork for each guest. After dipping and feasting, serve a crisp green salad and/or fruit.

1 1/2 lbs. Swiss or Emmentaler cheese, shredded
4 T flour or 2 T cornstarch
3 cups dry white wine
2 garlic cloves
1/2 t salt
pinch of pepper
dash of nutmeg (optional)
2 T kirsch
French, Italian, or sourdough bread, in bite-size pieces

IF USING FLOUR: Dredge cheese with flour. Set wine over low heat. When air bubbles rise to surface, but before wine boils, stir in cheese little by little. Be certain each addition has melted before adding more. Stir until bubbling gently. Set a fondue pot on alcohol flame or heating unit. Rub bottom and sides with peeled garlic clove. Add seasonings and kirsch to cheese mixture, blend, pour into fondue pot, and let the feast begin! Keep the fondue bubbling gently.

IF USING CORNSTARCH: Mix cornstarch and kirsch in small cup. Rub fondue pot with peeled garlic, put in the shredded cheese and seasonings and pour warmed wine directly over cheese, stirring constantly until cheese is melted. Blend in cornstarch mixture and cook 2 to 3 minutes, stirring, until fondue begins to bubble. Gently stirring when dipping the bread cubes helps keep the mixture well blended and also accumulates more fondue on the bread. Lift out cubes of bread with a twirling motion. Serves 6 to 8.

Ed. Note: For additional Fondue recipes, see the Fondue Cookbook, by Callahan.

PIRAGIES

Piragies are Russian potato-and-cheese-filled turnovers. They are related to the Pirog, a roll of yeast dough filled with chopped meat, hard boiled eggs, and/or vegetables such as cabbage and carrots. If Piragies seem too bland for your palate, add a bit of mashed garlic to the filling.

8 potatoes
1/4 lb. (1 cup) grated cheese*
salt and pepper to taste for filling, and 1 t salt for dough
4 cups flour
1/2 cup melted butter
2 T melted butter
1 1/2 large onions, grated
2 large eggs
3/4 cup milk

FILLING: Peel and boil potatoes until tender. (Dice for faster cooking.) Drain. Mash with 2 T butter, cheese, onion, salt, and pepper.

DOUGH: Mix eggs, flour, and salt, adding milk gradually while kneading until dough holds together. Roll out to 1/4 inch thickness and cut 5-inch diameter circles. Fill. Fold in half, seal edges with water and press with tines of a fork.

COOKING: Fry in remaining 1/2 cup melted butter until golden brown. (Or boil in salted water 15 minutes, then drain). Serve with additional fried onions. Serve as hot as possible. Piragies may be fried ahead and reheated in a warm oven. Makes about 25 turnovers.

*Cheddar, Parmesan, Romano, Dry Monterey Jack, or Edam.

 # KNISHES

The knish is a Jewish meat or cheese turnover—absolutely delicious for snacks or as a main course after (or with) vegetable soup. I think they are best served straight from the oven, but I have been successful making them ahead and reheating in a warming oven.

DOUGH:

1/2 t salt
1/2 lb. butter or margarine, melted
1/4 cup warm water
2 1/2 cups flour

2 eggs, beaten
1/4 cup sugar
2 pkg. dry yeast

Dissolve yeast in warm water. Beat eggs and mix with salt, shortening, sugar, and dissolved yeast. Add flour gradually and mix well. Cover and chill for 2 hours.

Roll out dough (half at a time) and cut with a 3-inch round cookie cutter.

Place about 1 T filling on each round, top with another round, and seal by crimping the edges together with the tines of a fork.

CHEESE FILLING:

1 egg	1/2 lb. farmers cheese
1 T sour cream	1/2 lb. cream cheese
2 T margarine or butter	sugar to taste
1 medium onion, chopped finely	

Fry onions in shortening until transparent. Mix with remaining ingredients. Use filling as directed above. Bake filled turnovers on lightly greased baking sheet at 350° for 25 minutes or until lightly browned.

CROQUE MONSIEUR

The Croque Monsieur is a hot cheese and ham sandwich served with a cheese cream sauce. A simplified version would be a grilled cheese sandwich with a slice of ham added, and no sauce; but here is the traditional method.

8 thin slices white sandwich bread
4 thin slices of ham
about 1 cup grated Swiss cheese,
    Emmentaler, or natural Gruyere

heavy cream
1 or 2 eggs, beaten
butter

SAUCE:
1 T butter
1 t flour
1 cup light cream

2 T grated Swiss cheese
salt and pepper to taste

60

SANDWICHES: Trim crusts from bread. Mix Swiss cheese with just enough heavy cream to make a thick paste, and spread a generous layer of it on each piece of bread. Put pairs of bread slices together, cheese in, with ham in the middle. Dip into beaten egg and sauté in hot butter until crisp and golden on both sides. Makes 4 sandwiches.

SAUCE: Blend melted butter with flour. Stir in cream gradually with cheese. Salt and pepper to taste. Let thicken slightly, stirring constantly, and serve over the hot sandwiches.

NOTE: Make the sauce ahead and keep it warm over hot water while sauteéing the sandwiches.

Cheese Sauces

England has three sauces and 360 religions, but France has three religions and 360 sauces.*

—Talleyrand

    *The numerical estimate of France's sauces is always varied. One modern French food writer estimates the number at about 3,000. In any case, it is the sauce that makes the chief difference between family cooking and haute cuisine in France—and it can make the same difference for you and yours.

BASIC CHEESE SAUCE

MEDIUM:
2 to 3 T butter
2 to 3 T flour
1 cup milk
1/8 t pepper
1/4 t salt
1/2 cup sharp American or
    cheddar cheese, grated

THICK:
4 1/2 T butter
4 1/2 T flour
1 cup milk
1/8 t pepper
1/4 t salt
1/2 cup sharp American or
    cheddar cheese, grated

(This is simply a white sauce with cheese added.)

Melt the butter over low heat in a heavy saucepan. Blend in flour. Cook over low heat about 2 minutes, stirring constantly, until mixture is smooth and bubbly. Stir in pepper and salt. Remove from heat. Stir in milk gradually. Return to heat, bring to a boil. Boil 1 minute—stirring constantly. Stir in cheese until melted.

VARIATIONS: For vegetable, rice, macaroni, and egg dishes, add 1/4 t dry mustard with the seasonings. For example, see Eggs with Cheese Sauce on following page.

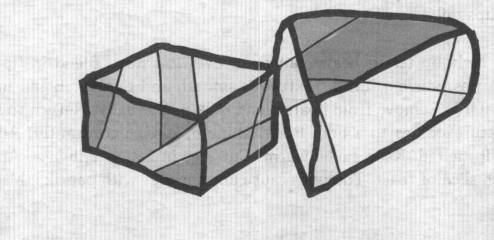

 # EGGS WITH CHEESE SAUCE

9 T butter
9 T flour
1/2 t salt
1/4 t pepper
1/4 t dry mustard
2 cups milk

1 cup grated, sharp cheddar or
  American cheese
8 hard-cooked eggs
8 slices toast, buttered
paprika

Melt butter in heavy saucepan over low heat. Blend in flour. Cook about 2 minutes, stirring, until mixture is smooth and bubbly. Blend in salt, pepper and mustard. Remove from heat. Blend milk in gradually. Return to heat and stir until mixture comes to a boil. Boil 1 minute, stirring constantly. Add cheese and stir until melted. Keep sauce warm. Cut eggs in half lengthwise. Arrange 2 halves on each slice of toast. Top with sauce and sprinkle with paprika. Makes 4 servings.

cheese sauce, page 66
8 oz. elbow macaroni
paprika or bread crumbs

Make cheese sauce using the same ingredients and directions as given in the Eggs With Cheese Sauce recipe on page 66. Cook macaroni according to package directions. Drain well and combine with cheese sauce. Transfer to buttered baking dish. Sprinkle with paprika or crumbs. Bake at 350° for 40 minutes. Serve immediately. Makes 6 to 8 servings.

VARIATIONS: 1) Add 2 bouillon cubes along with the milk when making sauce. 2) Cut cheese sauce recipe in half, but double the amount of cheese. Add 1 cup sour cream. 3) Add 1 1/4 t dry mustard and 12 oz. cubed ham to sauce.

BROCCOLI DOMINGO

2 lbs. broccoli
4 1/2 T butter
4 1/2 T flour
1/4 t salt
1/8 t pepper
dash cayenne

1 1/2 cups light cream
1/4 cup grated Parmesan or
  Swiss cheese
1 cup finely diced cooked ham
1 cup chopped stuffed olives
1/8 t nutmeg

Wash and trim broccoli leaving stalks 3 to 3 1/2 inches long. If thick, slash stalks for even cooking. Set aside. Melt butter in saucepan over low heat. Blend in flour. Cook, stirring, until smooth and bubbly. Add salt, pepper and cayenne. Remove from heat. Blend cream in gradually. Return to heat and stir until mixture comes to a boil. Boil 1 minute, stirring constantly. Stir in cheese until melted. Add ham, olives and nutmeg. Remove from heat and keep warm. Cook broccoli, uncovered, in boiling salted water until stems are just tender, about 5 minutes. Drain well. Arrange on ovenproof serving dish. Pour sauce over broccoli. Sprinkle with more cheese. Broil until golden. Makes 4 main dish servings.

CAULIFLOWER WITH CHEESE SAUCE

1 small cauliflower
Basic Cheese Sauce (medium), page 63
paprika, chopped parsley

Wash cauliflower and separate into flowerets. Cook in boiling, salted water until crisp-tender, about 10 minutes. Make sauce while cauliflower cooks. Drain cauliflower well and place on heated platter. Top with sauce. Sprinkle with paprika and parsley. Serve at once. Makes 4 servings.

# BASIC SAUCE MORNAY

To glamorize leftover meat, hash or eggs, place in a flat, oven-proof dish. Spoon Mornay Sauce over the top and broil until nicely browned.

4 1/2 T butter   1 cup milk
4 1/2 T flour   1 cup cream
1/4 t salt   1 cup grated, sharp cheddar,
1/8 t pepper   Swiss or Parmesan cheese
1/8 t cayenne pepper

Melt butter in a heavy saucepan over low heat. Blend in flour. Cook over low heat about 2 minutes, stirring constantly until mixture is smooth and bubbly. Blend in salt, pepper and cayenne. Remove from heat. Blend milk in gradually. Add cream. Return to heat and stir until mixture comes to a boil. Boil 1 minute, stirring constantly. Add cheese and stir until melted.

ENRICHED SAUCE MORNAY

Before making Basic Mornay Sauce (page 70), heat the cream with 1 bay leaf. Remove bay leaf when cream is hot. Then follow the basic recipe but increase the flour used to 6 1/2 tablespoons and add 1 tablespoon sherry and 1 egg yolk along with the cheese. Stir until cheese is melted. This sauce goes well with chicken.

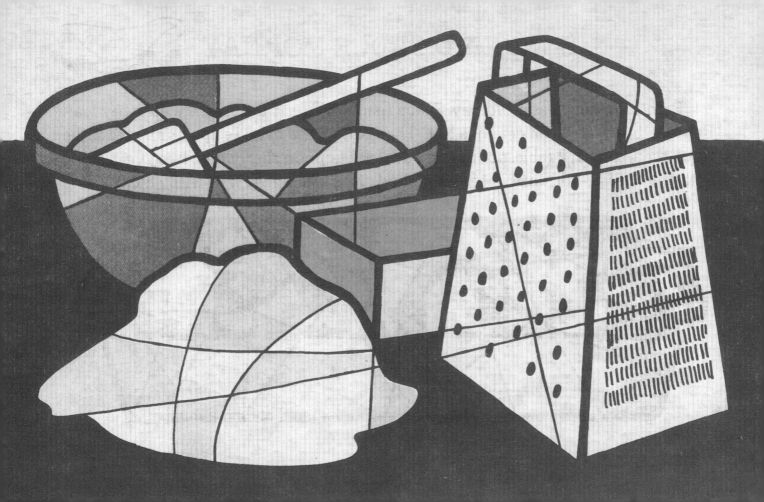

VEGETABLES WITH SAUCE MORNAY

Put cooked, drained, slightly under-cooked vegetables such as Brussels sprouts, carrots, cauliflower, green beans or boiling onions into a buttered casserole. Cover with Mornay Sauce (page 70). Bake at 350° about 20 minutes.

FILET OF SOLE MORNAY

Lay filets of sole in a buttered casserole. Spoon Enriched Sauce Mornay (page 71) of Basic Sauce Mornay (page 70) made with fish stock instead of milk, over top. Bake at 400° for 10 to 15 minutes or until fish flakes and the sauce bubbles gently at the edges. Serve immediately. Filet of halibut is also good prepared this way.

 # CANNELLONI

1/2 lb. ground veal	1 pkg. (3 oz) cream cheese
1/4 lb. ground beef	1/4 cup Parmesan cheese
1/4 lb. ground pork	1 egg, slightly beaten
olive oil	1 or 2 garlic cloves, minced
Enriched Sauce Mornay, page 71	1/2 t basil
Cannelloni dough, page 75	salt and pepper to taste
1 pint ricotta cheese	1/4 cup minced parsley

Have meat ground twice so it will be very fine. Brown in a small amount of olive oil. Drain off fat and cool meat. While meat is cooling make sauce and dough according to directions given. Add remaining ingredients to cooled meat and mix thoroughly. Spread about 2 tablespoons of filling on each square of cooked dough. Roll tightly and place layers in shallow baking dish. Spoon sauce over cannelloni and sprinkle with Parmesan if desired. Bake at 375° for 15 to 20 minutes or until thoroughly heated. Makes 4 to 6 servings.

DOUGH

2 cups flour
3/4 t salt
2 large eggs
1 1/2 T water

Sift flour and salt together into bowl. Add eggs and mix with fingers until dough can be gathered into a ball. Add water. Knead dough until very stiff, adding more flour if needed. Divide dough into three parts. Roll each third into a paper-thin sheet. Cut into 4-inch squares. Cook 6 squares at a time in 4 quarts boiling, salted water for 5 minutes, or until tender. Drain and fill as directed.

CHICKEN MORNAY WITH BROCCOLI

Mornay Sauce with Wine, page 77
1 pkg. (10 oz.) frozen broccoli spears
2 cups diced cooked chicken
2 T Parmesan cheese
chopped parsley

Make sauce as directed. Cook broccoli only until crisp-tender. Drain and arrange in a shallow 1 1/2 quart baking dish. Scatter diced chicken over broccoli. Pour sauce over all. Sprinkle with Parmesan. Bake at 425° 15 minutes or until bubbly. Sprinkle with parsley. Serve immediately. Makes 4 servings.

SAUCE MORNAY WITH WINE

4 1/2 T butter

4 1/2 T flour

1/4 t salt

1/8 t pepper

1 cup chicken broth

1/2 cup heavy cream

1/2 cup dry white wine

1/8 t Worcestershire sauce

1/2 cup grated Parmesan cheese

Melt butter in heavy saucepan over low heat. Blend in flour. Cook, stirring, until smooth and bubbly. Stir in salt and pepper. Remove from heat. Blend broth in gradually. Add cream, wine and Worcestershire sauce. Return to heat and stir until mixture comes to a boil. Boil 1 minute, stirring constantly. Add cheese and stir until melted.

# ORIENTAL LOBSTER MORNAY

Special Mornay Sauce, page 79
2 cans (1 lb. ea.) bean sprouts
2 cans (5 to 6 oz. ea.) lobster, drained
1 can (5 oz.) water chestnuts, drained
1/4 cup slivered green pepper
2 T grated onion
1/2 cup chow mein noodles
1 T butter

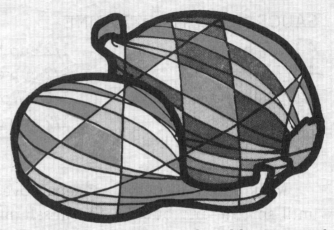

   Make sauce and set aside until needed. Rinse bean sprouts with cold water and let drain thoroughly in colander. Flake lobster and slice chestnuts. Add to sauce along with green pepper, bean sprouts and onion. Stir gently until mixed. Pour into a buttered 1 1/2 quart casserole. Sprinkle noodles over top. Dot with butter. Bake at 350° 25 minutes. Make 6 servings. Use crab instead of lobster, if desired.

78

SPECIAL MORNAY SAUCE

1/4 cup butter
5 T flour
1 t salt
1/4 t pepper
2 cups milk
1/2 cup light cream
2 t soy sauce
1 cup grated Swiss cheese

Melt butter in heavy saucepan over low heat. Blend in flour. Cook, stirring, until smooth and bubbly. Stir in salt and pepper. Remove from heat. Blend milk in gradually. Stir in cream and soy sauce. Return to heat and stir until mixture comes to boil. Boil 1 minute, stirring constantly. Add cheese and stir until melted.

Salads & Vegetables

There is something almost magic about salad. Like a hot bath after hard physical labor, a cool salad refreshes and invigorates the palate. Cheese blends with salads and vegetables and the wide variety of available cheeses makes it possible to experiment with taste sensations.

Tiny cubes of your favorite cheese are a welcome addition to almost any salad, vegetable dish or relish plate. Most of the recipes which follow are for main dish salads which, served with crusty bread and generous amounts of butter, provide a nourishing repast.

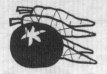

HAM SALAD BALLS

Serve these Ham Salad Balls with potato salad as a luncheon or supper main dish. (For an unusual potato salad, follow the recipe for Swiss Cheese Salad, but omit the cheese and eggs.)

2 cups finely ground cooked ham
1 cup dry cottage cheese
1 T horseradish
dash of tabasco sauce

1 T prepared mustard
1/2 cup commercial sour cream
1 cup finely snipped watercress
1/4 cup snipped fresh chives

In a large bowl, combine the ham, cottage cheese, horseradish, mustard, tabasco, and sour cream. Shape mixture into 12 balls about the size of an egg.

Combine watercress and chives. Roll balls in this green mixture until well-coated. Place on a tray, cover with plastic wrap, and refrigerate until serving time. (Should be served same day they are made.) Makes 12 balls, 4 servings of 3 each.

PARMESAN DRESSING

2/3 cup mayonnaise   1/3 cup milk   1/4 t Worcestershire sauce
1/3 cup grated Parmesan   1 t white wine vinegar

Blend thoroughly. Serve on mixed greens. Makes 1 cup.

LIME COTTAGE CHEESE DRESSING

1/2 cup mayonnaise   1 T sugar
1/2 cup small curd cottage cheese   1 T lime juice and 1/2 t grated rind
2 T milk

Mix ingredients thoroughly. Refrigerate, covered, until serving time. Serve on citrus fruit salad. Also compliments papaya. Makes 1 cup.

SALADE DE ANZA

This salad with Roquefort and blue cheese in the dressing is a favorite of my husband. Since blue/Roquefort dressings are so popular, two more recipes follow.

4 medium garlic cloves, crushed
1/4 cup olive oil
3 oz. Roquefort cheese
1 oz. blue cheese
1 cup salad oil or olive oil
1/3 cup cider vinegar
1/4 cup wine vinegar

1 t salt
1/2 t sugar
1 t paprika
lettuce, cherry tomatoes, artichoke hearts, and cucumber slices, in proportions and amounts you wish

Using a blender or fork, crush the garlic and mix very thoroughly with the olive oil. Add cheese gradually, making a smooth paste.

Mix salad oil, vinegars, salt, sugar, and paprika. Add cheese paste and mix well. Store in refrigerator in a covered jar until serving time.

Serve on crisp lettuce. Garnish with tomatoes, artichoke hearts, and cucumber slices or wedges. Makes 2 cups of dressing.

ROQUEFORT DRESSING

1 cup mayonnaise
2 to 4 oz. Roquefort cheese
1 cup light cream

1 t salt or garlic salt
1/2 t paprika

Mash cheese and add mayonnaise gradually. Mix in rest of ingredients. Refrigerate in covered jar until serving. Makes about 2 cups.

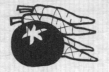

MOLDED ROQUEFORT SALAD

A molded cheese salad is very unusual, particularly when it becomes a main dish, the center filled with a seafood salad. What to serve with it? A cold marinated vegetable (artichoke hearts, cooked string beans, asparagus, mushrooms), white wine, and lots of crusty bread and butter.

1 envelope unflavored gelatin
1/4 cup fresh lemon juice
1 cup boiling water
1/4 lb. Roquefort cheese
1 cup grated or finely chopped cucumber
1 cup heavy cream
your choice of seafood salad: tuna, crab, salmon, shrimp (try mixing one
   carrot, peeled and grated, into salmon salad)
parsley and paprika for garnish

4 T minced fresh parsley
2 T minced pimiento
1 T minced capers
1 t grated onion
salt and pepper to taste

Soften gelatin in lemon juice for 5 minutes. Then combine with boiling water and stir until dissolved.

Mash Roquefort and then combine with cucumber, parsley, pimiento, capers, onion, and season to taste. Stir in gelatin. Refrigerate. When it just begins to gel, whip the heavy cream in a chilled bowl with a chilled beater, and fold into gelling cheese mixture.

Rinse a 6-cup ring mold with cold water or coat lightly with oil. Spread the cheese mixture evenly in the mold. Chill for 4 hours or until firm.

SERVING TIME: Unmold ring on a chilled serving platter. Garnish with parsley sprigs around outer edge. Fill center with cold seafood salad and sprinkle with paprika. Serve at once. Makes 6 servings.

CHEESE SALAD

1 large head of lettuce (red leaf or butter)
1/2 lb. cheese, cut into matchstick slivers (Samsoe, Edam, Gruyere, or Swiss)
2 hard-boiled eggs, peeled & quartered

DRESSING:
1/2 cup sour cream
6 T milk or light cream
1 T Dijon mustard
1 T fresh lemon juice
1/4 t basil
1/4 t cumin seed
1/4 t tarragon
1/4 t salt

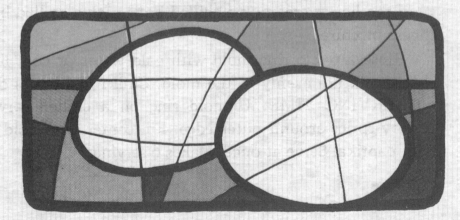

Beat together all dressing ingredients. Cover and chill until ready to use.

Wash, drain, and chill lettuce.

At serving time: Tear lettuce into bite-sized pieces into a bowl. Top with cheese slivers and egg quarters. Pour over dressing and mix at table. Makes 6 to 8 servings.

This salad is delicious with cold or hot roast beef, or steak. A dry red wine will go nicely with beef and this salad.

VARIATION: To make this salad qualify as a main dish, add 2 or more cups of julienne strips of cold roast beef. You may need to increase the sour cream, or add a little mayonnaise to cover this added ingredient. A few cold string beans are good, too. Serves 6.

SWISS CHEESE SALAD

The Swiss are fond of combining potatoes and cheese in one meal. Here is that combination in a main-dish salad.

1 lb. (4 or 5 small) potatoes
salt
vinaigrette dressing
1/2 lb. aged Swiss cheese, diced (2 cups)
1/2 cup diced celery hearts
3 T minced green onion
3 T minced fresh parsley
4 eggs, hard-boiled and peeled
2 slices bacon, cooked crisp and crumbled
1/2 cup mayonnaise
freshly ground pepper

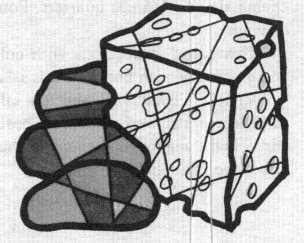

Peel, or do not peel scrubbed potatoes, as you wish. Dice into medium-size pieces. Cook in boiling salted water until just tender but still hold their shape. Drain. While hot, sprinkle with 4 T dressing. Cool, then combine with cheese, celery, onion, 2 T of the parsley, 3 eggs—chopped, and the bacon.

Mix mayonnaise with the remaining dressing. Thin with a little vinegar, if necessary, and pour over salad. Toss lightly, season with pepper, and chill.

To serve, finely chop remaining egg and mix with remaining parsley. Sprinkle over top of salad. Makes 6 servings.

VINAIGRETTE DRESSING:
Beat together until combined:
6 T olive oil   1/4 t dry mustard
2 T vinegar   dash of freshly ground pepper
1/4 t salt

SCALLOPED POTATOES WITH CHEESE

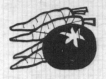

2 lbs. potatoes, thinly sliced after peeling
grated Parmesan, Swiss, or mild cheddar cheese
salt, pepper and nutmeg to taste

3 minced cloves of garlic
3 T butter
pint of light cream

Make layers of potato slices in a large, shallow baking dish which you have buttered. Sprinkle with salt, pepper, nutmeg, and garlic.

Bring the cream just to a boil. Pour over potatoes and dot top with butter. Bake at 350° for 1 3/4 hours.

Sprinkle top with grated cheese to taste (at least 1/2 cup). Adjust heat to 400° for 15 more minutes. Serve at once.

This dish is excellent for entertaining, because you have plenty of time to prepare for your guests while it cooks. Nice with steak, plus asparagus cooked ahead and marinated for a few hours in vinaigrette (see p. 91), then served on lettuce. Serves 4 to 6.

93

MASHED POTATOES WITH CHEESE

1/4 cup butter or margarine
1/2 cup peeled and coarsely chopped onion
6 medium potatoes, peeled, diced, cooked and drained
3/4 cup warm milk*
1/2 cup pasteurized process cheese spread
3/4 t salt
1/4 t pepper

Cook and drain potatoes. Melt butter in a small saucepan, add onion, and saute until lightly browned. Whip the hot potatoes in the large bowl of an electric mixer, adding warm milk gradually. Continuing to whip, add butter, onions, cheese spread, salt and pepper. Whip until fluffy and serve at once. Serves 6.
*Hate to warm milk because it boils over easily? Simply mix powdered instant dry milk with the amount of hot water required to make 3/4 cup reconstituted milk.

GREEN BEANS DANISH STYLE

2 lbs. fresh green beans   paprika
1/4 cup melted butter   4 oz. Danish Danbo, Samsoe, or Tybo cheese, grated

Wash the beans well. Cut off the tips with a sharp knife. Put the beans in a large flat kettle with a tight lid, adding 1 cup cold water and a dash of salt. Cook the beans over high heat at first. When the water is boiling rapidly, turn the heat down and cover tightly. Simmer 18 to 20 minutes, or until the beans are cooked but still firm.

Meanwhile, melt the butter. In the top of a double boiler, melt the grated cheese.

When the beans are done, drain. Put them on a warm serving platter. Dribble the melted butter over them, sprinkle with paprika (and some freshly grated pepper, if you wish.) Then pour the melted cheese over the beans and serve at once with cold cuts, roast beef, lamb, chicken, or turkey. Serves 6.

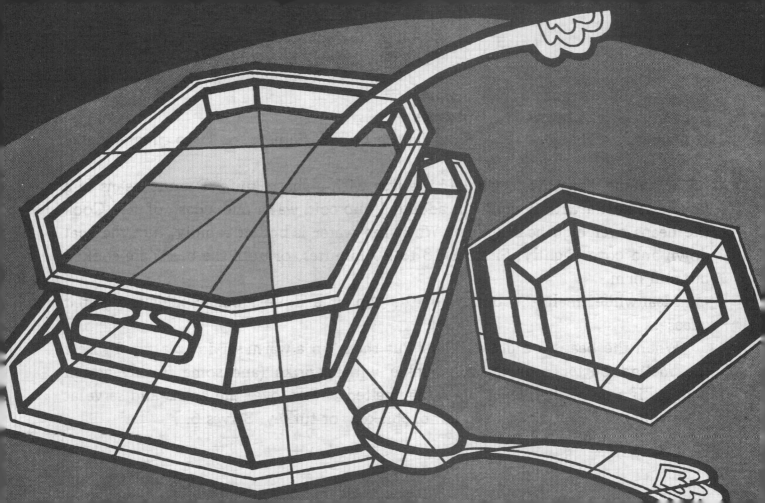

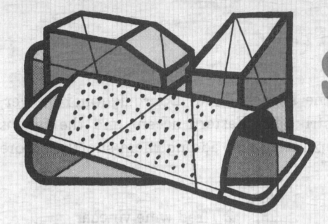

Soups & Stews

Ah! la bonne odeur de soupe au fromage!
—Alphonse Daudet.

For a simple "soup with cheese," serve as a first course hot, clear, homemade chicken broth, each serving topped with a teaspoon of either Romano or Parmesan. Or add cheese to your soups with croutons of buttered bread sprinkled with cheese, cubed and fried or baked slowly. (Remove crusts first.) Shredded, grated or cubed cheese can be used as a garnish for almost any soup or stew.

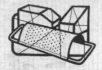

GREEK-STYLE STEW

This Greek-Style Stew is similar to the French Boeuf Bourguignon; however, cinnamon, cloves, raisins, and cumin strike an Eastern accent and the feta is definitely Greek. Cooking the onions separately and adding them shortly before the stew is done prevents flavor "loss."

3 lbs. lean stewing beef, cubed
salt and pepper, to taste
1/4 cup olive oil
2 1/2 lbs. small white onions (about 1" diameter)
1 T butter
2 oz. tomato paste
1 cup (8 oz.) tomato sauce
1/2 cup red wine
1/4 to 1/2 lb. feta cheese, cut into small cubes

2 T red wine vinegar
1 T brown sugar
3 cloves garlic, mashed
1 bay leaf
1 small cinnamon stick
1/2 t ground cumin (optional)
8 whole cloves
2 T raisins or currants
3/4 cup walnut halves

Preheat oven to 350°. Season meat with salt and pepper. Heat oil in a Dutch oven or heavy kettle, then add meat and coat with the oil but do not brown. Mix together tomato paste, tomato sauce, wine, vinegar, brown sugar, cumin and garlic. Pour over meat. Add bay leaf, cinnamon stick, cloves, and raisins (tied in a square of cheesecloth for easy removal after cooking), cover and bake in the oven for 2 1/2 hours.

Remove from oven and take out bay leaf, cloves and cinnamon stick. Gently stir in walnuts, cheese, and onions. Simmer on top of stove about 10 minutes. Serve with bread to dip into the sauce.

ONIONS: Peel. To keep them from bursting during cooking, make an X 1/4" deep in the root ends. Place in one layer in a heavy saucepan or skillet. Add 1 T butter and 1/2 t salt and enough water to cover onions about halfway. Cover and simmer slowly for 20 to 30 minutes, until tender. Drain and proceed as above. Makes 6 servings.

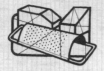

SOUP WITH CHEESE

1 quart homemade broth (chicken, pork, or beef; chicken necks are good
   for making stock)
1 T butter
2 T minced fresh chives
1 cup finely chopped celery and its leaves
1/2 t tarragon
1 T fresh minced parsley
1 small onion, finely diced
salt and pepper to taste
1/3 cup dry white wine
soppers: 6 slices dry toast (made with thick slices of French bread if possible)
garnish: 6 t grated Romano, or Parmesan, or dry Monterey cheese

Melt butter and add chives, celery, parsley, and onion. Cook very slowly 5 minutes. Add rest of seasonings and stir well. Add broth, cover, bring to the boil, then reduce heat and simmer for about 20 minutes, or until vegetables are tender. Taste, and add more salt and pepper if necessary. Soup may be set aside for a few hours at this point if you wish.

To Serve: Heat, then add wine. Put a piece of toast in each soup dish, ladle some soup over the toast, and top with cheese. Serve at once. (Butter toast first if you wish, but toast need not be hot as soup will warm it.) Makes 6 generous servings.

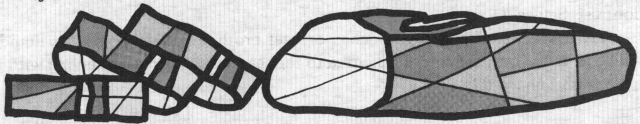

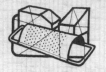# CHEDDAR SOUP

2 cups (8 oz.) shredded cracker-barrel cheddar
1/2 cup shredded carrot
2 T chopped or grated onion
1/4 cup butter or margarine

1/3 cup flour
1 t salt
dash of freshly ground pepper
4 cups milk

Saute carrot and onion in butter. Stir in flour, salt and pepper. Gradually add milk, stirring, and cook until thickened, stirring occasionally. Add shredded cheese and stir until melted. Do NOT boil. Serve with a garnish of croutons or a bowl of popcorn on the side. Cucumber or celery sticks will also provide crunchy contrast. Serves 4.

VARIATION: Use 3 cups chicken or beef broth, and 1 cup milk for liquid. Add 1/2 t dry mustard and 1 t paprika to the seasonings. Top each serving with a little fresh minced dill.

CHEDDAR SHRIMP SOUP

1 medium onion, chopped
2 T butter or margarine
3/4 cup boiling water
4 medium potatoes, diced
1/3 cup diced celery
1 1/2 t salt
1/4 t pepper

1 lb. fresh cooked, or canned, shrimp
1 cup half & half, heated
2 cups milk, heated
1 cup shredded cheddar cheese
1/4 cup sherry
1/3 cup chopped chives

Saute onion and celery in butter until tender. Add boiling water, potatoes, salt and pepper. Cover and simmer about 20 minutes or until potatoes are cooked but still firm. Add shrimp, hot milk and hot half & half. Heat thoroughly, then add cheese and stir slowly until all cheese is melted. Add sherry, stir, and put into individual bowls. Garnish with chopped chives and serve. Serves 6.

VEGETABLE SOUP WITH CHEESE

This soup is made entirely with canned ingredients, except for the spinach and onion—and the spinach could be a leftover from a previous meal. If you wish, make it entirely with fresh vegetables.

10 1/2 oz. condensed beef broth (canned or homemade)
2 cups cooked whole tomatoes, crushed (1 lb. can, or home-cooked)
1 1/4 cups water
1 T cornstarch
9 oz. pkg. Italian green beans, cooked and drained
1 cup sliced cooked carrots
1 cup large shell macaroni, cooked and drained
1/2 cup coarsely chopped cooked spinach
1/2 cup onion slices
2 T butter or margarine

1 or 2 cloves garlic, minced
1/4 cup grated Parmesan cheese

Sauté onion and garlic in butter until lightly browned.

Mix cornstarch with water; combine with broth and tomatoes in a large saucepan. Cook, stirring, until thickened. Add vegetables, sauteed onion, garlic, and cheese. Season with a little basil and pepper if you wish. Heat. Serve with additional cheese and chewy bread. Serves 6.

VARIATION: Substitute 1 cup raw chopped cabbage for the carrots. Saute with the onion and garlic, covered, for about 10 minutes. The moisture in the cabbage is sufficient for this type of cooking.

Main Dishes

Are you concerned about rising food costs, particularly those of meat? Consider using cheese at least once a week as the protein source in a main dish. If a pound of cheese costs you $1.09, each half pound—or 54 1/2¢ worth—will yield 2 cups of grated cheese, enough for most main dishes! To make potato soup a main dish, stir in 1/3 cup grated cheddar; stir until melted. Try scalloped potatoes with cheese added, omelets or scrambled eggs with cheese—or any of the following recipes.

Some Salads and Sandwiches in this collection may be considered Main Dishes.

STEAK WITH BLUE CHEESE

Blue cheese complements beef. For this marinated steak, flank, London broil, or chuck are good choices. (A sirloin should not be insulted by additives.)

1/3 cup white wine vinegar
1/3 cup water
2 T soy sauce
1 onion, sliced
1 clove garlic, mashed
freshly ground pepper
1 1/2 lbs. steak
1/4 cup crumbled blue cheese

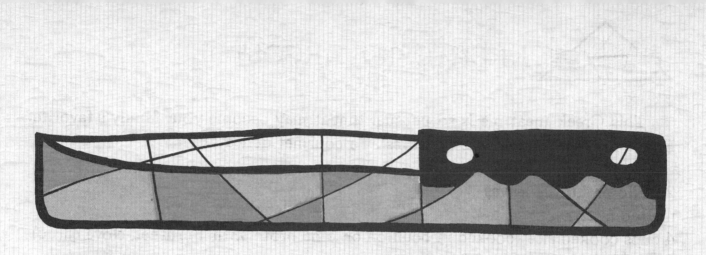

For marinade, combine vinegar, water, soy sauce, onion, garlic, and pepper. Score steak lightly on both sides and marinate at least six hours, turning occasionally. Use a non-metal, shallow dish for marinating. If marinating overnight, steak should be put in refrigerator and covered.

Place steak on broiler pan or over coals (about 4 to 5 inches above coals), and broil 5 to 7 minutes. Turn and sprinkle with blue cheese on cooked side. Broil second side until cooked as you wish. Place on a platter, and slice into thin diagonal slices across the grain. Makes 4 servings.

KREATOPITA ARGOSTOLI

This Greek meat pie is so unusual that it may become your family's favorite. Buy a package of Filo pastry leaves at a gourmet delicatessen.

24 Filo or strudel leaves
melted butter
4 cups cooked rice (cooked in bouillon or lamb broth with 1 crushed clove garlic)
3 cups cubed, roasted lamb
lemon juice
1 cup cooked, diced potatoes
4 hard-boiled eggs, quartered
1 T grated lemon peel
2 T fresh mint
2 T fresh parsley
2 T lemon juice

1 1/2 cup crumbled feta cheese

1/2 cup olive oil

1 cup bouillon or lamb broth

1 t salt

1/2 t pepper

1/2 t oregano

1 beaten egg

Butter and line a 14 x 10 x 2" baking pan with 12 Filo leaves (about half a package), adding 1 leaf at a time and spreading each with melted butter, using a pastry brush.

Top with mixture of cooked rice, cubed lamb sprinkled with lemon juice, potatoes, eggs, lemon peel, mint, parsley, lemon juice, feta, olive oil, broth, salt, pepper, oregano, and beaten egg.

Top with 12 more pastry leaves, adding in same manner as bottom crust.

Bake at 250° for 2 hours, or until pastry is browned. Serves 10.

 LASAGNE

1/2 lb. ground beef
1 cup chopped onion
2 large cloves garlic, minced or crushed
2 t oregano
2 cans (10 3/4 oz. each)
  condensed tomato soup

1/2 cup water
2 t vinegar
1/2 lb. plain lasagne noodles,
    cooked and drained
1 pint cottage or ricotta cheese
1/2 lb. mozzarella cheese, thinly sliced

Cook lasagne noodles according to directions on package. Replace hot water with cold and let stand while preparing filling.

In frying pan, brown beef and cook onion, garlic, and oregano. Add soup, water, and vinegar. Simmer 30 minutes, stirring occasionally.

In a baking dish, 12 x 8 x 2", arrange 3 alternate layers of noodles, cottage cheese, meat sauce, and mozzarella. Bake at 350° for 30 minutes. Let stand 15 minutes before serving. Makes 6 servings.

PASTITSIO

This is a Greek macaroni and meat casserole, similar to the Italian Lasagne, but with the Eastern touch of cinnamon and nutmeg. Delicious for a buffet.

6 T butter
1 lb. ground beef
1 lb. ground lamb
1 large chopped Bermuda onion
1/2 cup white wine
1/3 cup tomato paste
1/2 t cinnamon
1/2 t nutmeg
1 1/2 t salt

1/2 t pepper
1 chopped fresh tomato
1 beaten egg
1/4 cup fine bread crumbs
1 lb. macaroni (your choice of shape)
3/4 cup grated Parmesan cheese
white sauce (See page 116)
tomato sauce (See page 117)
bread crumbs, butter

Brown the beef, lamb, and onion in butter. Add the wine, tomato paste, cinnamon, nutmeg, salt, pepper, and chopped tomato. Simmer, stirring, 5 to 8 minutes. Cool slightly, then stir in beaten egg and bread crumbs.

Cook macaroni according to package directions and drain well.

Butter a 12 x 12" baking dish. Sprinkle bottom with bread crumbs. Put in half the macaroni. Cover with 1/4 cup grated cheese. Add the meat mixture. Cover with another 1/4 cup cheese. Add remaining macaroni, top with white sauce and sprinkle with remaining cheese. Dot with butter and bake at 400° for 35 minutes. Serve with tomato sauce. Serves 8.

NOTE: May be refrigerated before cooking. In this case, you may need to increase the heating time to 45 minutes.

# WHITE SAUCE

5 T butter   1/4 t nutmeg
5 T flour   1/4 t cinnamon
2 1/2 cups hot milk 3 egg yolks
1 t salt

    Cook as any sauce, stirring until thickened. Remove from heat. Stir in nutmeg, cinnamon and egg yolks. Return to heat; cook until thickened.

TOMATO SAUCE

8 T butter
1 clove minced garlic
2 minced medium size onions
2 t chopped carrot
4 1/2 cups canned tomatoes
1/2 t basil

1/2 t pepper
3/4 cup water
1 t oregano
1/2 t salt
1 cup dry white wine

Heat butter. Brown the onion, garlic, and carrot. Then mash in the canned tomatoes using a fork; cook 2 to 3 minutes, stirring. Add seasonings, wine, and water. Cover and simmer 40 minutes. Uncover and puree or rub mixture through a strainer. Simmer about 15 more minutes. Serve over hot Pastitsio.

NOTE: Prepare this the day before, refrigerate, then reheat at serving time.

# BASIL PASTA SAUCE

If you don't like tomato-ey sauce, try this basil and cheese one, similar to a "pesto."

3 cloves garlic, minced
1 bunch parsley, finely chopped
3 large branches fresh basil, or 2 teaspoons dried
1/3 cup sweet butter
3 oz. cream cheese
3 oz. blue cheese
3/4 cup olive oil
6 t grated Parmesan cheese
salt and pepper to taste

Mash the garlic, parsley, and basil with the butter, cream cheese, and blue cheese. Add olive oil gradually. Then add Parmesan and season to taste. Serve over hot pasta. Will keep in refrigerator overnight, tightly covered. Serves 6.

VARIATION: Substitute 1 1/4 cups grated Parmesan for the Parmesan, cream cheese and blue cheese; and stir in 1/3 cup finely ground pine nuts or walnuts with the Parmesan. Enough for about 1 pound of hot cooked spaghetti.

119

# FETTUCINE ALFREDO

Fettuccine (noodles) Alfredo is a favorite at my table. It can be served with a number of other dishes, such as pot roasts, cold tongue, or even broiled hot dogs.

1/2 lb. fine noodles
1/4 lb. unsalted butter, diced
3/4 cup freshly grated Parmesan cheese

1/4 cup heavy cream, warmed
1/2 t pepper

Cook noodles. Drain and put on hot serving dish or platter, or in chafing dish over spirit lamp or flame. Add remaining ingredients and toss quickly but thoroughly. Cheese and butter should melt into a creamy sauce that coats noodles. Use large serving fork and spoon as if you were tossing salad. Makes 4 servings, side dish.

STUFFED MUSHROOMS WITH CHEESE

Some stuffed mushrooms are suitable only as appetizers. These, however, with their meat, cheese, and spinach stuffing, are definitely a main dish. They can be prepared ahead, refrigerated, and put in the oven to bake when your guests arrive—ready in 25 minutes.

2 lbs. fresh spinach (or equivalent frozen)
1 cup sour cream
1/2 cup grated cheddar
1/2 cup grated Monterey Jack
1/2 cup grated Parmesan cheese
1/4 cup chopped green onions
1/2 t salt

1/2 t oregano
2 cloves garlic, minced
12 large fresh mushrooms,
    washed and stems removed
1 lb. ground chuck
1 t salt

TOPPING:
1/2 cup shredded cheddar
1/2 cup Monterey Jack, shredded
sprinkling of nutmeg

Wash mushrooms, remove and chop stems. Put mushrooms, cup (stem) side up, in center of a larger shallow baking dish.

Cook spinach briefly in hot water. Drain well and chop. Mix with sour cream, cheeses, salt, and oregano, then spoon mixture around edges of mushrooms.

Saute ground beef lightly with onions, garlic and 1 t salt. Spoon over mushroom caps. Top with cheese and nutmeg. Cover. Bake at 350° for 25 minutes. Makes 4 servings.

THE SECRETS OF SOUFFLÉS

1) Allow egg whites to sit at room temperature for one hour before using to achieve maximum volume when whipping.

2) Make sure your utensils are clean and grease-free.

3) Use a copper bowl, because the chemical reaction between copper and albumin makes the foam sturdier. If you have no copper bowl, 1/4 t of cream of tartar for every 4 egg whites has the same effect.

4) Give the soufflé something to cling to as it bakes. For main dish soufflés, butter the dish and coat with finely grated Parmesan or Swiss cheese, or fine dry bread crumbs. (For desserts, butter and coat with granulated sugar.)

5) Serve the souffle as soon as baked. (It may stand up to an hour before baking.)

124

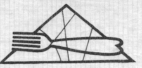

5 egg whites
4 egg yolks
1 t butter
2 T grated Parmesan cheese
3 T butter
3 T flour
1 cup hot milk
1/2 t salt
1/4 t dry mustard
few grains cayenne (optional)
1/4 t Worcestershire sauce
1 cup coarsely shredded cheddar cheese (1/4 lb.)

Bring egg whites to room temperature. Then heat oven to 400° Butter a straight-sided 1 1/2 quart casserole or souffle dish with the t of butter; sprinkle bottom and sides evenly with the Parmesan cheese.

Melt 3 T butter in a saucepan over low heat. Add the flour and stir, cooking for 2 minutes. Remove from heat and beat the milk in gradually, until mixture is thickened and smooth. Stir in salt, mustard, cayenne, and Worcestershire. Return to heat and cook 1 minute, stirring constantly, or until very thick. Remove from heat and beat egg yolks in one at a time. Pour into a large bowl.

Beat whites until stiff but not dry. Add 1 large tablespoonful of the whites to the egg yolk mixture and stir in well. Add all but 1 T of the cheddar. Slide remaining egg whites from bowl onto the egg yolk mixture, and fold in with a rubber spatula; do this gently to retain as much of the air in the beaten whites as possible. Pour into the prepared dish. Level the surface and sprinkle reserved cheese over top. Run a metal spoon or spatula through the mixture in a circle 1 inch from the edge of the dish, as if tracing the brim on a hat.

Bake in center of oven, reducing temperature to 375° as soon as soufflé is put in. Bake 35 to 40 minutes, or until soufflé is puffed about 2 inches above the rim of the dish and a knife inserted in one side comes out clean. Serve immediately. Makes 4 servings.

VARIATIONS: 1) The cheese may be increased to 1 1/2 cups. 2) Use instead of Parmesan, any one of the following: Blue cheese, Roquefort, Gruyere, Emmentaler, or Provolone; or use half Swiss and half Parmesan.

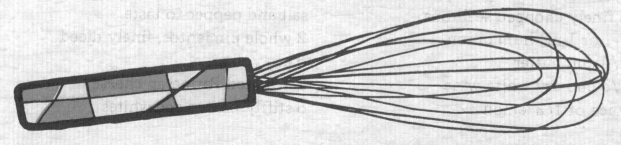

ZUCCHINI SOUFFLE

Zucchini, a variety of summer squash developed in Italy, is a rather bland vegetable, especially as it gets older and larger. For the most flavor buy young zucchini, about 6 inches in length or less, and combine them with garlic, white wine and Parmesan to make a wonderful soufflé, a specialty of the Blue Fox in San Francisco. (Because of all the eggs, this is a main dish.)

1 lb. young zucchini
1 or more cloves garlic, crushed
3 finely chopped scallions,
    or 1 medium onion
1/4 cup butter
2/3 cup dry white wine
juice of 1/2 lemon

1 T chopped fresh parsley (or 1 t dry)
pinch of nutmeg
salt and pepper to taste
2 whole pimientos, finely diced
6 egg yolks
2 T grated Parmesan cheese
6 stiffly beaten egg whites

Remove the tops and bottoms of the zucchini. Cut remaining unpared vegetable in pencil-thin strips lengthwise, then crosswise in 1-inch pieces.

Sauté the crushed garlic and scallions (or onion) in butter until they begin to look limp. Add zucchini pieces; cook for 2 minutes more, stirring constantly. Add the wine, lemon juice, parsley, nutmeg, salt, and pepper. Cook briskly until almost dry and zucchini is tender, stirring occasionally to prevent sticking. (A Teflon-lined pan is a help in preparing this recipe.) Add diced pimientos, mix, and set aside to cool.

Beat egg yolks with cheese until yolks are thick and lemon-colored. Add cooled zucchini. Fold in stiffly beaten egg whites. Pour into a well-buttered casserole or baking dish; place in a pan of hot water. Bake at 400° for 25 minutes, or until firm and fluffy. Serve at once. Makes 6 to 8 servings.

EGGPLANT PARMESAN

1 large eggplant, or 2 medium size
2 cups bread cubes, crusts removed
1 cup grated sharp cheddar or
    Parmesan cheese
6 slices bacon

4 eggs
1 cup milk
1 T butter or margarine
1/4 cup grated Parmesan or
    Romano cheese

Peel eggplant and dice into cubes 1 or 1/2 inch square. Place in rapidly boiling water to cook crisp—not soft. Drain. Mix with bread cubes, 1 cup cheese, and fried and crumbled bacon. Beat together eggs and milk; pour over eggplant mixture in buttered 3-quart casserole. Dot with butter, sprinkle with the grated cheese and as much of the bacon fat as you wish. Bake at 325° until custard is set when tested with knife blade—about 45 minutes. Makes 4 to 6 servings.

QUICHE LORRAINE

The following Quiche is delicious hot, at room temperature, or cold. Serves 4 to 6 as a main dish. For hors d'oeuvres, cut into smaller wedges, serves 10.

1 deep 10-inch pie plate lined with
   pie crust or puff pastry
1/4 cup finely chopped white or
   green onions
1 1/2 T butter
1 cup crumbled, crisp-cooked bacon
   (or finely diced cooked ham)
5 eggs

1 egg yolk
2 1/2 cups light cream
1/8 t nutmeg
1/2 t salt
2 dashes cayenne pepper (optional)
dash white or black pepper
1 cup grated good quality Gruyere or
   Swiss cheese

CRUST: Line a 10-inch pie plate with your favorite pie crust or puff pastry. Bake 8 to 9 minutes at 400°. This is a partial baking and may be omitted.

FILLING: Cook onions in butter until transparent. Mix with bacon or ham and set aside. Beat eggs and yolk lightly; blend in cream, nutmeg, salt, cayenne, and pepper. Put meat and onions into pie crust. Top with grated cheese and pour egg mixture over all. Bake 30 to 35 minutes at 375° or until the filling is golden and puffy, or until a knife inserted into the custard's center comes out clean.

VARIATIONS: 1) Replace Gruyere or Swiss with 1/2 cup crumbled Roquefort or 1/2 cup softened cream cheese. 2) Replace onions with 2 T minced chives. 3) Replace onions with chopped leeks and bacon with garlic-flavored sausage, chopped. 4) Replace bacon with cooked shrimp or crab meat. 5) Omit meat and add some freshly cooked peas, chopped spinach or endive, or increase onions to 1 1/2 cups. 6) Use a small can of deviled ham instead of bacon. 7) Greek variation known as Tiropeta: use milk instead of light cream, and substitute 2 cups (1 lb., crumbled) Feta for the Gruyere. Omit bacon and onions.

FLORENTINE PIE

This Italian main dish pie is related to the French Quiche. It is a medley of vegetables and, if you omit the bacon, is a vegetarian dish. The cheese is all in the crust; however, you may reduce eggs to 2 and add 1 cup grated cheddar cheese to the filling.

1 1/2 cups thinly sliced onion
8 slices bacon, diced
10 oz. pkg. frozen peas and celery
  OR 1 cup cooked peas and 1/4 cup sliced celery
1/2 cup light cream

1/2 t salt
dash of pepper
1/2 cup milk
3 eggs, slightly beaten

Saute bacon in a skillet until crisp. Remove and drain on absorbent paper. Saute onion in bacon fat until transparent but not browned. Remove and drain.

Cook frozen peas and celery. Bring cream, milk, salt, and pepper to a boil in saucepan. Reduce heat and pour a small amount of this hot mixture into the beaten eggs. Add eggs to hot mixture, stirring constantly, until slightly thickened. Stir in peas, celery, onions, and bacon. Pour into Cheese Crust. Bake at 400° for 15 minutes, reduce heat to 325° and bake 15 minutes longer, or until knife inserted 1" from center comes out clean. Cool slightly before serving.

CHEESE CRUST:

1 cup grated cheddar cheese	1/4 t dry mustard
3/4 cup flour	1/4 cup melted butter
1/2 t salt	

Mix with pastry blender or fork until smooth. Knead about 1 minute. Press firmly onto bottom and sides of 9" pie plate and flute edge of crust. Serves 6.

AUSTRIAN PANCAKES

(with Cream Cheese Filling)

BATTER:
2 cups milk
2 eggs
2 cups flour
pinch of salt
vegetable oil for frying

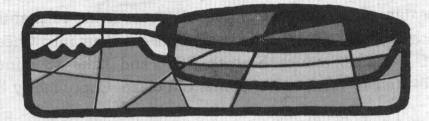

Sift the flour, with a pinch of salt, into a bowl. Stir in one egg and half the milk; mix well. Repeat. Allow batter to rest for half an hour before using.

Spread a little oil around your skillet to coat and heat. Turn the pan as for a crepe after you have put in a little batter, so that it covers the bottom of the pan and you will have a thin pancake. Flip only once. Keep warm while you fry all the cakes. Fill and roll up; place side by side on a warm dish, sprinkle with sugar, and serve at once.

May be filled with apricot jam, a mixture of grated nuts and sugar, or the following Cream Cheese Filling.

CREAM CHEESE FILLING:
1/4 cup raisins, finely chopped
2 egg yolks
4 T butter, softened
grated rind of 1 lemon
1/3 cup sugar
8 oz. cream cheese

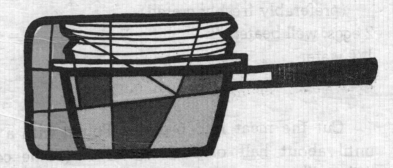

Mix all ingredients thoroughly and spread pancakes with this mixture. Keep plate of filled pancakes over a pot of simmering water or in a warming oven while filling the rest of them. Serves 4.

VEAL PARMESAN

2 lbs. boneless veal cutlets, about 1/2" thick
1 1/4 cups fine, dry bread crumbs
1/2 cup Parmesan cheese, grated
   (preferably freshly grated)
2 eggs, well beaten
1 T water
1 t salt

1/4 t pepper
1/3 cup olive oil
   (or half butter, half olive oil)
2 cans (8 oz. each) tomato sauce
1/4 lb. fresh mushrooms
1/2 t rosemary
6 slices (3 oz.) mozzarella cheese

Cut the meat into 6 pieces. Pound with a wooden mallet, or potato masher until about half original thickness. (Some cooks say they should be almost "filmy.")

Combine bread crumbs and Parmesan cheese.

Mix together eggs, water, salt, and pepper.

Heat oil in large heavy skillet. Chop mushrooms, or slice thinly. Saute lightly and remove from skillet.

Dip cutlets into egg mixture and then into crumb mixture. Brown in skillet; pour tomato sauce over cutlets, return mushrooms to skillet and top cutlets with mozzarella slices. Simmer, covered, 10 minutes or until cheese has melted and is lightly browned. Serve at once. (This dish should not be prepared ahead.) Serve with plain pasta or rice and a tossed green salad. Serves 6.

VARIATIONS: 1) Mash a whole clove of garlic into the oil when you heat it. Remove clove just before you pour on the tomato sauce. 2) Replace mushrooms with 1 onion, sliced. 3) Replace 1/2 cup of the tomato sauce with 1/2 cup white wine. 4) Replace rosemary with 1/2 teaspoon thyme.

SALMON CHEESECAKE

Salmon Cheesecake is a delicate mousse made in a spring form pan: light but satisfying—perfect for a summer luncheon.

1 1/2 cups unsweetened
   zwieback crumbs
1/4 t nutmeg
6 T melted butter
2 envelopes unflavored gelatin
1/2 cup cold water
2 eggs (large), separated
1/2 t salt

1 can (7 3/4 oz.)
   good quality salmon, flaked
2 cups heavy cream
grated rind of 1 lemon
2 T lemon juice
2 cups creamed cottage cheese
1/2 cup milk

CRUST: Combine crumbs, nutmeg, and melted butter. Press about 3/4 of the crumb mixture onto bottom and sides of a buttered 7 1/2-inch spring form pan, chill. Reserve remaining crumb mixture to sprinkle on top.

FILLING: Soften gelatin in cold water. In a small saucepan combine egg yolks, salt, and milk. Cook over low heat, stirring constantly, until egg mixture coats the spoon. Remove from heat, add gelatin and stir until gelatin dissolves. Set aside.

Press cheese through a sieve or beat thoroughly with an electric mixer or blender. Beat in lemon juice, grated rind, and egg mixture. Fold in flaked salmon.

Beat egg whites until stiff, but not dry, and fold into salmon-cheese mixture. Whip cream until stiff and fold in carefully. Spoon mixture into crust and sprinkle with reserved crumbs. Chill for several hours or until set.

To serve: Carefully remove sides of pan and place the "cake" on a serving platter. Serve with finger sandwiches—watercress, cucumber, tomato—on buttered whole wheat bread for texture contrast. Serves 4 to 6.

Desserts

You may not have thought of it before, but your main dish need not necessarily be the one with the protein content in your menu. Why not the dessert? When serving onion or mushroom soup—neither of which is high in protein, but will contain goodly amounts of vitamins—serve a high protein dessert like cheesecake. American homemakers usually plan a protein in the main dish, but this is not nutritionally necessary, and it is sometimes easier on the budget to reverse the order of things. The next time you contemplate minestrone, gaspacho, ratatouille, or zucchini souffle for your main dish, consider cheese for dessert.

Of course one of the most delicious desserts — and one with little preparation —is fruit in season served with a wedge of cheese.

JEWISH NOODLE KUGEL

Many of us use rice for both main dishes and puddings, but somehow never do the same "switch" with noodles. For the cook who likes to add a new dimension to her cuisine upon occasion, the following pudding is ideal. It's especially appropriate after a vegetarian main dish. (Some cooks serve this with meat, as a side dish, but I find that combination too rich.)

3/4 t salt
7 1/2 oz. (approx.) farmer cheese
1/2 lb. egg noodles (medium or narrow)
3 eggs, beaten
1 1/2 cups unsweetened applesauce
    (preferably homemade)

grated rind and juice of 1 lemon
1/2 cup sugar
1 T melted butter
1 cup sour cream
1/2 cup diced dried apricots (optional)

Cook noodles following package directions. Drain and rinse with cold water to keep noodles from sticking together.

In a bowl combine eggs, applesauce, lemon juice, grated rind, cheese, sugar, salt, and melted butter, with apricots. Gently fold in drained noodles. Mix thoroughly. Add sour cream and blend.

Put into a greased baking dish and bake at 350° for 45 to 60 minutes, or until set. Serve warm or cool.

VARIATIONS: 1) Omit applesauce and substitute 1 1/2 cups crushed pineapple. 2) Substitute 1/4 cup golden raisins for the diced apricots. 3) Separate eggs. Beat egg whites until stiff. In a separate bowl, beat yolks until thick and lemon-colored. Fold yolks, then whites, into the noodle mixture. Makes 6 to 8 servings.

FEUILLETES AU GRUYERE

Feuillettes au Gruyere (leaves with Gruyere) is a Swiss pastry, a kind of cheese strudel. Rich and delicious.

STRUDEL DOUGH:
2 1/4 cups flour
2 beaten eggs
1/4 cup melted butter
1/2 t salt
6 to 8 T lukewarm water

FILLING:
2 cups grated natural imported Gruyere cheese
2 beaten eggs
2 T melted butter
1/2 cup heavy (whipping) cream

BASTE:
1/4 cup melted butter or heavy cream

For dough, sift flour into a bowl. Mix in eggs, butter and salt, then stir in enough lukewarm water to make the dough hold together. Knead 10 to 15 minutes, without adding more flour, until dough is no longer sticky. Cover and let dough rest about 1/2 hour.

For filling, mix together all ingredients thoroughly.

When dough has rested, sprinkle a large pastry cloth with flour and roll out the dough on it until paper thin. Spread the dough with the filling. Use the cloth to help roll the strudel up like a jelly roll. Transfer to a buttered baking sheet. Cut into pieces or make into a coil. Bake at 350° until golden, basting frequently with melted butter or cream.

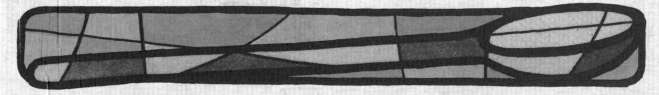

 # PASHKA

Pashka is a creamy cheese dessert, traditionally made in Russia for Easter. Originally it was made in a pyramidal mold, but it can be made in any mold you have or shaped with your hands into a cone. The Russians decorate their pashka with candied fruits and almonds, spelling XB ("Christ is Risen" in Russian) on one side, and a cross on the other side.

3 cups large-curd cottage cheese
4 T sweet butter, at room temperature
1 cup whipping cream
2 egg yolks
1/2 cup sugar
1/3 cup chopped candied fruits
1/2 cup finely chopped almonds

Sieve the cottage cheese, then mix with softened butter.

Heat whipping cream to boiling point and set aside.

Beat egg yolks and sugar for 3 minutes with an electric mixer. Slowly add cream to eggs. Put into a saucepan and cook over low heat until mixture thickens, stirring constantly. Remove from heat and stir in fruits and almonds. Place the pan in a large bowl of ice cubes and stir until cold.

When cream mixture is cold, add to cottage cheese-butter mixture.

Line a mold with one or two layers of damp cheese cloth; press mixture into mold. Refrigerate overnight. Remove from mold and decorate just before serving. Serves 8.

BLINTZES

The blintz is a Jewish pancake related to the Russian blini (served at Shrovetide) and the French crepe. The blintz is presently popular as a dessert.

BATTER:

1/2 cup clarified butter

5 eggs

1 1/4 cups cold water

1 cup all-purpose flour

2 T sugar

1 t salt

To clarify butter: melt it very slowly, remove any foam from top, and pour off golden liquid, discarding solids in bottom of pan. Measure out 1/2 cup of clarified butter.

Pour eggs, water, salt, sugar, and flour into a blender or mixing bowl. Blend or beat until very smooth, then pour into a bowl (if using blender).

Heat a heavy skillet (about 7 inches in diameter) over a moderate flame. Brush skillet with butter. Pour just enough pancake batter (about 3 T) into skillet to coat bottom. Sauté until pancake is light mottled brown on bottom; do not brown top. Remove to a towel and stack. Continue until all batter is used.

FILLING:

12 oz. farmer cheese	2 t lemon juice	3 T sugar
6 T sour cream	6 oz. whipped cream cheese	1/4 t salt

Mix all ingredients until well blended. Place about 3 T filling on the browned side of each blintz. Roll up, tucking in ends, to form blintzes. Cover with clear plastic wrap and chill in refrigerator until serving time. Then sauté blintzes in clarified butter until medium brown on both sides. Use two skillets, if necessary. Serve with sour cream and jam such as blueberry, wild strawberry or bar-le-duc (red currant). Serves 4.

INDIAN SWEETMEAT

If you like to travel to foreign lands at your dinner table, prepare a chicken curry and a bowl of saffron rice. Serve with little dishes of condiments for your family to add to their curry if they wish, singly or in combination: flaked coconut, peanuts, raisins, chutney. For dessert serve an authentic Indian cheese sweet, and fresh fruit.

3 1/2 cups unsalted farmer or ricotta cheese
1 1/2 cups powdered sugar
1/2 t ground cardamom

Sieve or blend cheese until smooth. Place in a saucepan. Add sugar and mix well. Heat, stirring constantly, until mixture leaves side of pan. Add cardamom. Remove from heat and turn onto a flat dish or tray. Form into leaf shapes or small balls while hot. Serve warm or cold. Serves 6.

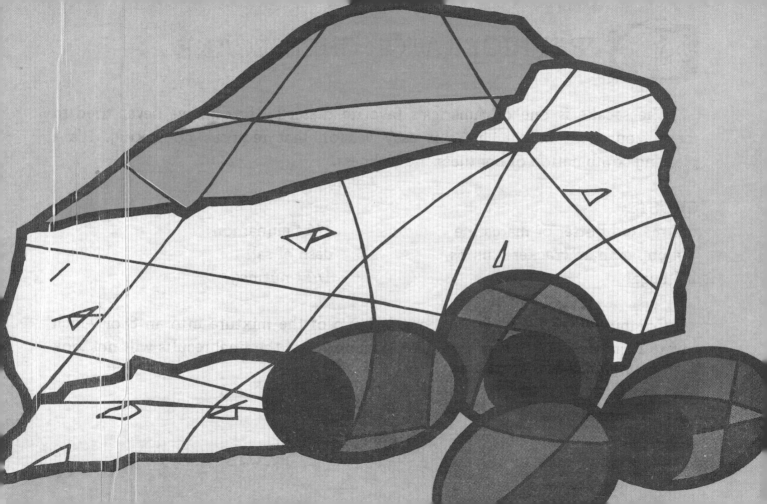

# REFRIGERATOR CHEESECAKE

Cheesecake is one of America's favorite desserts. If you have never tried to make your own before, try this easy version that requires no baking. It's a pleasing combination of lightness and richness.

CRUST:
3 T melted butter or margarine
3/4 cup graham cracker crumbs
2 T sugar

1/4 t cinnamon
dash of salt
1/4 t nutmeg

Combine ingredients. Press about 1/2 cup of the mixture into an 8 or 9-inch spring form pan. (You can use a pie plate; however, the final results will not look as decorative when you serve it.)

FILLING:

2 envelopes (2 T) unflavored gelatin
1 cup sugar
2 eggs, separated
1/8 t salt
1 T lemon juice

1 t grated lemon rind
1 cup milk
1 t vanilla
3 cups (24 oz.) creamed cottage cheese
1 cup whipping cream, whipped

Mix gelatin, 3/4 cup sugar and salt in a pan. Beat egg yolks and milk together. Stir into gelatin mixture. Put over low heat; stir constantly until mixture thickens slightly. Remove from heat. Add grated rind, lemon juice, and vanilla. Chill, stirring occasionally, until mixture mounds slightly when dropped from spoon.

Sieve or beat cottage cheese until smooth. Stir into gelatin mixture. Beat egg whites until stiff; gradually add remaining sugar and beat until glossy. Fold into gelatin mixture. Fold in whipped cream. Turn into crust and sprinkle with crumb mixture. Chill until firm. Remove sides of spring form and serve. Serves 12.

PINEAPPLE CHEESECAKE

This is very like the British Trifle, a dessert of cake-and-jam crust with custard poured into the middle. With convenience foods, it's a very easy dessert to make. Sometimes called "Tipsy Pudding"—when it includes lots of sherry. Sprinkle your jelly roll slices with sherry, about 2 tablespoons, if you wish.

5 small jelly rolls, thinly sliced
1 pkg. (3 oz.) vanilla pudding & pie filling mix (the kind that must be cooked)
2 envelopes unflavored gelatin
2 cups milk
2 eggs, separated
16 oz. (2 cups) whipped cream cheese
1 can (about 9 oz.) crushed pineapple
1/4 cup sugar
1 cup heavy cream, whipped

Place enough jelly roll slices around sides of a buttered 8-inch spring-form pan to line completely; place remainder in bottom. (The traditional Trifle uses a rounded bowl, and you might find that easier.)

Mix pudding mix and gelatin in a saucepan; beat in milk and egg yolks. Cook, stirring constantly, until mixture reaches the boil; slowly beat into cream cheese using a large bowl. Stir in pineapple and its syrup. Chill, stirring often, until mixture mounds lightly.

Beat egg whites until foamy. Then beat in sugar until meringue stands in firm peaks. Fold meringue into gelatin mixture, then fold in stiffly whipped cream. Pour into prepared pan. Chill until firm--3 to 4 hours. Remove side of pan, cut into wedges and serve. Makes 12 to 16 servings.

 # CRÈME DE CAMEMBERT

This is a luxurious dessert. Serve with French bread and red wine. Or you might prefer "water biscuits" (large, plain crackers) instead of bread.

1 ripe Camembert
dry white wine to cover
about 1 cup very fine toast crumbs (made from stale bread dried slowly
   in the oven)
1/3 cup unsalted (sweet) butter

Scrape off the skin of the Camembert. Cut the cheese into chunks or sections and put into a bowl. Cover with dry white wine and let stand at room temperature for 12 hours. Drain. Dry the pieces with cloth or paper towels. Put into a bowl and cream thoroughly with butter. Shape this crème into the form of the original cheese. Coat with the fine crumbs and chill before serving. Serves 6.

158

Cheese
Guide

STORING CHEESE

Fresh cheese—cream cheese, ricotta, Neufchatel, cottage, Coeur a la creme—should not be stored more than a few days, as they are intended to be consumed fresh. Therefore, buy only what you will eat and refrigerate promptly, tightly wrapped in either the original paper or plastic wrap.

The soft but ripened or fermented cheeses, such as Pecorino (a sheep's milk cheese), Brie, Stilton, Camembert, Boursault, Boursin, can be kept up to a week, refrigerated, in plastic wrap or a tightly sealed plastic bag or you can use a cheese keeper. (See Cheese keeper, page 165.)

The hard, fermented cheeses, like aged Cheddar, Edam, Emmenthal, Gorgonzola, Dry Monterey, aged Parmesan or Romano, may be stored in several ways. Wrap in cloth moistened with salt water, white vinegar, or white wine, and store in a closed container in your refrigerator. Change the cloth every 3 or 4 days. Or wrap in waxed paper, seal in a plastic container, and freeze; or dip in brandy, wrap in plastic, then foil (Parmesan won't need to be refrigerated after this brandy treatment; Swiss will).

A GLOSSARY OF CHEESES AND CHEESE TERMS

NOTE: Charles de Gaulle once said in a fit of pique, "How can you expect to govern a country that has 246 kinds of cheese?" Other estimates put the number of French cheeses alone at over 400, and some sources have counted a world total of over 1000.

A bulletin of the New York State College of Home Economics "counts" cheeses another way, coming up with a total of 18 distinct types, which differ from one another in kind of milk used, amount of fat and water retained in the curd, and the flavor and texture produced during ripening.

How were the cheeses included here chosen? I sent out questionnaires to friends and relatives from Oregon to Wisconsin and Maine to Florida. The cheeses available to them are, I assume, available to you, and are included here.

American cheese—a softish-solid, mild cheese, white to pale yellow, similar to Cheddar.

Asiago—an Italian cheese, mild when soft, sharp when older and harder. Good for any occasion.

Bel Paese—a popular Italian cheese, now made in the U.S. to exact Italian specifications. Creamy, soft, mild, light yellow with slate grey exterior. Essentially a dessert cheese.

161

Bierkase or "Beer Kaese"—a pungent German cheese, intended for consumption with beer.

Bleu—any French blue cheese.

Blue—robust American or British imitation of Roquefort, generally cream colored with blue or blue-green mottling, piquant flavor, and smooth, rich buttery texture. The mottling is a result of innoculation with Roquefort penicillin mold. Complements: fruit and crackers for snacks or desserts. Recommended: Oregon Blue, Maytag (from Iowa), Stella.

Bonbel—a soft, bland French cheese, resembling American Muenster. Melts smoothly. A dessert cheese. Complement: Mandel Bread (a Jewish cookie).

Boursin—a creamy, elegant, slightly sweet dessert cheese. It and its siblings (Boursault, Petit Suisse, Crema Dania) complement: bread, bland crackers, fruit (pears, apples, grapes, peaches, El Dorado plums, bananas). In herbed or peppered form, Boursin complements: cold vegetables and meats.

Breakfast—a small, fresh, white cheese, soft, with a ripened butter flavor. Resembles Continent's Fruhstuck, Lunch, Delikat, and Lauterbach. Complements: toast & jelly, pineapple, peaches and grapes. Recommended: Rouge et Noir (Petaluma, CA).

162

Brick—a semi-hard, aromatic, elastic, yellow American cheese, with a strong, sweetish taste, shaped like a brick; small eyes. Good for toasted sandwiches or with plums.

Brie—a soft, fermented cheese made from raw curds and believed by many to be the world's most elegant cheese. Famous since the 15th Century. Recognized as a "royal cheese" at the Congress of Vienna in 1815. Has an edible tan crust with a few traces of powdery white. Made in wheel form. A Brie is fully ripe when pressure exerted on the crust causes the cheese to bulge but not run. The cheese itself should be creamy and pale yellow. A winter cheese, available November to May. Complements: melon, grapes, nectarines, plums. Wine experts say, "Serve Brie with a red."

Broach—to tap, pierce, or open; said of casks of wine, bodies of enemies, subjects of conversation, and large cheeses. In France a whole cheese is offered first to the master of the house, who drives a knife into it before handing it around--so that guests will not hesitate to "dig in."

Camembert—a soft, aromatic cheese "created" in 1761 by Marie Harel, in the hamlet of Camembert, France. Later "discovered" by Napoleon. Made from whole milk and aged on trays of straw. Has an edible yellowish crust similar to that of Brie, but wheels are smaller and thicker. Delicate in flavor when ripe, but can be offensively ammoniacal when past its prime. (Sample before buying.) Complements: grapes, apples, or graham rusks and jelly.

Cantal—a distinctive French cheese; golden, semi-firm, delicious. Eat out of hand and cook with it.

Caciocavallo—literally "horse cheese." An Italian and Balkan cheese originally made from mare's milk, but now from cow's, sheep's, and/or goat's milk. Firm, buttery, smoky—similar to Provolone.

Coeur a la creme—a delicate, soft, fresh French dessert cheese similar to cream cheese. Curds of naturally soured whole milk are mixed with cream and drained in heart-shaped wicker baskets. Complement: strawberries.

Cheddar—a hard, smooth, cheese, flaky when aged, and some shade of orange-yellow. It was originally made in Cheddar, England, and is aged 2 to 5 years before marketing. American cheddar varies in color from almost white to golden orange. Nicknames: rat cheese, cracker barrel cheese, Coon, Longhorn, Tillamook, and Rainier (available in Washington and Oregon only). Varies in flavor from mild to very sharp. Complements: apples and crackers, pasta.

Cheese—from the Latin caeseus, Anglo Saxon cese, and Middle English chese. A food made from the curd of milk or from whey, it keeps for extended periods of time at cool temperatures and combines well with almost any other food.

Cheese keeper—a glass container with a tight cover; grids on the bottom keep the cheese above a mixture of vinegar and water (1 T salt to 3 T each water and vinegar). The fumes from this mixture keep the cheese fresh and moist. Make your own keeper with a jar with a layer of marbles at the bottom.

Cheese rennet—yellow bedstraw sometimes used for coagulating milk to form cheese.

Cheshire—a very popular English cheese, very hard, made in two colors, orange-red and white. Complements: Red Beauty and Late Santa Rosa plums.

Colby—a semi-firm American Cheddar, made in Vermont.

Coon—a Cheddar made in New York state, white, sharp, usually coated with black waxed cloth.

Cottage cheese—a soft, white cheese made by straining and seasoning the curds of sour skimmed milk. Nicknames: Dutch cheese, pot cheese, smeerkaas. Very perishable; buy only from a cold cabinet and store promptly in your refrigerator.

Cream cheese—a fresh American cheese, never ripened. It has a confusing name, because this cheese is not made with cream, but is usually made from skimmed milk; then the curds are bathed with cream afterwards. "Double cream" is made using milk with some cream added before the rennet, and mixed with some cream after curdling. Avoid: the kind full of vegetable gum.

Creamed cottage cheese—prepared by adding cream to cottage cheese curds. For "tangy style" creamed cottage cheese, sour cream is used to bathe the curds; for "California style," sweet cream is added. Calories can range from 240 per cup and up.

Crema Dania—mild, delicate, and rich. Serve as dessert with a sweet fruit, like Bing cherries, or a cherry liqueur.

Coulommiers—a soft, pungent French cream cheese, consumed fresh. Has a white crust with slight greyish tinge.

Dry cottage cheese—does not have cream or milk around, or bathing, the curds.

166

<u>Dry Monterey</u>—a deep yellow, aged, grating cheese, very hard and sharp. (See "Monterey Jack.")

<u>Dutch cheese</u>—an Edam; also, another name for cottage cheese.

<u>Edam</u>—a mild, yellow-red Dutch cheese made in a round mold and fermented until a non-porous rind forms, then encased in red wax. (The Hoffman House, a San Francisco saloon in the '90's frequented by classy demimondaines, served free lunches noted for their variety and gourmet surprises. Daily menus featured a haunch of beef, a ham, sausages, broth, and an Edam cheese. The cheese had been scooped out, mixed with champagne, and then replaced in its shell.)

<u>Emmenthal, or Emmentaler</u>—a medium-hard cheese made in Switzerland and Austria; has larger eyes than Gruyere but is milder. Excellent in fondue or eaten in the German fashion: thin slices sprinkled with salt and pepper.

<u>Erbo</u>—an Italian cousin of Gorgonzola, the mildest of the Blues.

<u>Estrom</u>—a buttery, sweet, semi-soft Danish cheese.

Eyes—the "holes" in a cheese caused by fermentation when cheese is cured in a warm room. The size of the eye has nothing to do with either the quality or taste of the cheese. In "process" cheeses, eyes are produced artificially by chemical additives which simulate the effects of aging by causing violent fermentation.

Farmer's cheese—reminiscent of cottage cheese but with a higher fat content, finer curd.

Feta—one of the best known Greek cheeses; however, a great deal of the Feta marketed in the U.S. originates in Bulgaria. Feta is mild, flaky, slightly tangy, pure white, and made from sheep's/goat's milk. Comes in irregular chunks surrounded by its own briny whey. Complements: other Aegean products (ripe olives, olive oil, lamb).

Fondue—from the French word fondre, "to melt." A peasant dish of Switzerland consisting of cheese melted with white wine, seasoned with pepper and/or kirsch. Pieces of bread or cubes of boiled potato are swirled in the cheese and eaten.

Fontina, or Fontine—a round, mellow firm, white, Italian, Swiss, Danish, or American cheese; melts smoothly. Complements: wine or fruit.

Fromage Fondu Pour Tartine—a "Tartine" is a slice of bread spread with butter, jam, soft cheese—any spreadable substance. This type of cheese is sometimes seasoned with nuts (Parfume aux noix) or seasoned with cherry liqueur (Parfume au Kirsch). A dessert cheese.

Fruit—the Marin French Cheese Co. (Petaluma, CA) recommends "all fresh fruits, notably pears and apples" with cheese.

Gorgonzola—from a town of the same name, ten miles from Milan. This semi-hard, delicate Italian cousin of Roquefort should be yellowish white with blue veins and a thin rind. Semi-soft when young and flaky when mature. Italians call it Il Re de Formaggio ("the king of cheeses").

Gouda—an oblate or loaf-shaped cheese made in Holland from whole milk. Larger and richer than Edam.

Grating of cheese—experts say you'll get four times as much flavor if you grate your own rather than purchasing it already grated.

Gratin—the adjective applied to a dish which has been given a crisp, attractive, golden crust via a topping of bread crumbs and/or grated cheese, a dousing with melted butter, and quick browning under a broiler or with high heat.

169

Gratinée—in France this usually means "sprinkled with fresh or dried fine bread crumbs plus melted butter and quickly browned." In the U.S. it usually means "sprinkled with bread crumbs, grated cheese and browned."

Gruyere—a pungent, fermented, light-yellow cheese made from scalded curds. True Gruyere is made in the Gruyére valley in French-speaking Switzerland. Has smaller eyes than Emmentaler and keeps a long time unbroached.

Gruyére, process—a blend of shredded natural Gruyére and Swiss or Emmentaler, cooked together, then pressed into wedges and foil-wrapped.

Goat—imported from France and very expensive. In Portugal, goat cheese is eaten as dessert with fruit or marmalada (quince jam). Recommended: Ill de France, Valensay Pyramid, Montrachet.

Jack—see "dry Monterey" and "Monterey Jack."

Jarlsberg, Jarlsburg—a semi-soft Norwegian swiss cheese with large eyes.

Kashkaval—the Green or Rumanian version of Caciocaballo.

170

Kasseri—a hard cheese with a flavor between Parmesan and Cheddar.

Keeping hard cheeses—to preserve the freshness of hard cheeses: (1) wrap in waxed paper, seal in a plastic container and freeze; or (2) dip in brandy, wrap in plastic, then foil; Parmesan won't need to be refrigerated after this brandy treatment; Swiss will; or (3) the Swiss wrap a cloth soaked in white wine or salt water around chunks of Gruyére to preserve them.

Kummel—a Dutch cheese with caraway seeds; another name for Leyden.

Kumminost—pale yellow and flecked with caraway seeds.

Lappi—a Finnish Jack-type cheese.

Leyden—a Dutch hard cheese spiced with cumin, cloves, or cinnamon and made in same way as Edam.

Liederkranz—a domestic cheese, created by a German immigrant; name means "wreath of song." Golden yellow with a thin, edible crust, robust flavor and aroma. Complements: beer.

Limburger—a semi-hard, fermented cheese made in France, Belgium, Germany, and seasoned with chives, parsley, and tarragon. Although the flavor itself is mild, Limburger has a very distinctive odor, falling into a category my husband terms "old sock cheese." Creamy white with grey-brown exterior. Complements: tart apples, bland crackers, grapes.

Longhorn—a medium-sharp American Cheddar molded in cylindrical shape. Good for cooking.

Mold—if your cheese starts to grow some, use non-moldy part at once; or grate, wrap tightly, and freeze for later cooking use.

Monterey Jack—a domestic hard cheese, creamy in color with a delicious flavor similar to Swiss in its youth. First produced in Monterey County, CA. Melts smoothly. Recommended: Lady Lee (Lucky).

Mont St. Benoit—a Gruyére type cheese made by Benedictine monks. Use in fondues, casseroles, omelets, salads. Melts well. Good for dessert. Recommended: Hickory Farms (Abbey of Saint-Benoit-du-Lac, manufacturer).

Mozzarella—a hard but malleable Italian cheese; mild and delicious, creamy in color,

172

originally made of buffalo milk. Use in lasagne and pizza. Melts smoothly.

Munster or Muenster–the European variety is pungent and soft, with small eyes; the American version is semi-soft, delicious, mild, buttery, with an orange exterior. Complements: bananas, bread, butter, wine, and apples. Recommended: Lady Lee.

Neufchatel —a delicate cheese with a white crust prepared from sweet milk with or without cream added. Originated in Normandy. The American version is an unripened cheese similar to cream cheese.

New York Martin—a sharp Cheddar.

New York white—a sharp Cheddar.

Parmesan—known as grana in Italy because of its finely grained texture. Needs at least 2 years to mature. Parmesan is a popular hard, dry, yellow Italian cheese with a delicate and striking flavor. Sold in chunks or grated form, young Parmesan complements apples, grapes, or cantaloupe. Grated Parmesan is served in a small bowl with a spoon as a side dish with pasta. Each diner sprinkles spoonfuls over his food to taste.

Petit Suisse—a fresh (unfermented) cheese, creamy, unsalted. See "Boursin".

Pipo Crem—a mild blue cheese.

Pizza—a flat, over-size tart, is thought to have originated in Naples and has a base of raised dough topped with anchovies, tomatoes, oregano, sausage, shrimp or what have you. If cheese is used as topping, it is often mozzarella. Sophia Loren fries her pizza.

Pont-l 'Eveque—a soft cheese of Normandy, takes its unique flavor from a fungus peculiar to that region. Soft, pale yellow.

Popcorn cheese—same as "large curd cottage."

Port-Salut, Port-du-Salut, or Port Salude—a creamy, yellow, robust, whole milk cheese first made at the Trappist monastery of Port du Salut, France. Trappists still make this—from a secret recipe.

Pot style—cottage cheese made from skimmed milk and salt only. Fat content is usually under 1% and calories range from 160 to 200 per cup. Nicknamed "Dutch cheese."

Process cheese—two or more green cheeses (i.e., cheeses less than 1 year old)—or an expensive aged cheese—diluted with gum, water, powdered milk, etc. Process cheese lacks the quality and full flavor of aged cheese but is less perishable because of the additives. Popularized by James Kraft in the early 1900's. Do not employ as topping, because it melts into a gummy mass. Recommended: Cache Valley Smoki (from Utah).

Process cheese food—a blend of natural cheeses with other ingredients (such as non-fat dry milk, pineapple, pimientos, chives, whey, water) to a spreadable consistency. By law it must contain at least 51% cheese by volume.

Protein—The Milk Advisory Board reminds us that 3 oz. of cheese provide the same amount of protein as 3 oz. of meat, poultry, or fish; 3 eggs; 1 1/4 cups baked beans; or 3/4 cup cottage cheese. One ounce of cheese provides as much calcium as 3/4 cup of milk.

Provolone—one of Italy's best-known cheeses, easily recognized by its rope-tied form. Originally made of buffalo milk, it has a firm, smooth texture, and a smoky tang. Use for snacks or dessert, with crackers or fruit. Also good for cooking; melts smoothly.

Queen of cheeses—a title often assigned to Camembert.

Quiche—also called "Quiche Lorraine." A hot main-dish tart, native to Lorraine, France. (The Italians and Swiss have very similar dishes, however.)

Raclette—a Swiss dish made by heating a special softish white cheese before a fire or a raclette broiler, scraping off the softened side onto a warm plate, and eating with bread and/or small boiled potatoes.

Raw milk vegetarian cheddar—See Vegetarian cheese

Rennet—the catalyst of the chemical reaction that produces cheese. The rennet comes from the lining of a bovine's fourth stomach, and is objected to by some non-meat eaters. Actually many cheeses are curdled with the flowers and leaves of bedstraw (Galium verum) and would therefore be acceptable to all. Added to milk, rennet causes the milk's "solid" parts--the casein and most of the butterfat--to break away from the watery part—the whey— and form into a solid mass. See also "whey."

Ricotta—a soft, dry, white Italian cottage cheese, used in Manicotti, lasagne, and some desserts. The Italian variety is made of sheep's milk or whey left from another cheese made with sheep's milk; American Ricotta is made of skimmed cow's milk. Complements: brown sugar, chocolate, peaches, tomato sauce.

Romano—a yellowish-white, granular Italian cheese, similar to, but more strongly flavored than, Parmesan. Excellent for grating but too hard for cheese tray or dessert.

Room temperature—the way all cheese should be served for fullest flavor. Remove from your refrigerator 1 to 2 hours before serving. Warning: cheese that is repeatedly refrigerated and warmed, refrigerated and warmed, suffers; so take out only what you expect to consume.

Roquefort—the name is limited by French government regulations to blue cheese made with sheep's milk and cured in humid mountain caves in the Roquefort region. All genuine Roquefort bears the symbol of a red sheep. The blue veins peculiar to a Roquefort are a result of aging in the particular climate from which the cheese absorbs certain delicious micro-organisms. Complements: guava jelly, apples, unsalted wheat crackers, butter. Good for cooking.

Samso or Samsoe—a nut-like, buttery Danish cheese, made on the island of Samso. Golden, semi-firm, with small eyes. Complement: plums.

Schloss or Schlosskaese—strong flavored, yet mellow, golden cheese. Originating in Austria; its name means "castle cheese." Complements: dark rye bread and beer.

Small curd cottage cheese—has a tangier taste than large curd, the degree of tanginess depending on whether (or what type) cream is used to bathe the curds. Nicknames: "country style cottage cheese," "farm style."

Stilton—a rich, waxy, English cheese made from whole milk with cream added; has a good aftertaste. Marked with grey and green streaks of mold. To serve, scoop this cheese from the center rather than cut from the side of the wheel. If you wish, pour a little sherry or port on the top and allow it to soak in first. Traditionally, Stilton is served with port, after a leisurely, memorable meal.

Swiss—a delicious, hard, pale yellow cheese, full of eyes. Good in sandwiches, with ham and in many cooked dishes. Recommended: Safeway brand "natural Swiss."

Tillamook—a pungent, bright yellow, firm Oregon cheddar. All purpose.

Tilsiter or Tilsit—a semi-firm, piquant cheese. Imported from Germany, Poland.

Turophile—a "cheese lover." If you are a turophile, you are probably also an oenophile (wine lover).

Vegetarian cheese—contains neither rennet nor salt but is curdled with an enzyme.

Whey—the thin, watery, almost bluish part of milk, which separates from the solid part when rennet is added. Whey is often rich in butterfat and some cheeses (like the Scandinavian Primost) are made from it alone.

Wine—wine merchants have a saying, "Buy on bread, sell on cheese." This means that bread makes the palate more critical, more sensitive to a wine's imperfections, whereas cheese has the opposite effect. When serving wine to guests, if unsure of its quality, serve cheese to make it taste better! To make your cheese taste its best: with Camembert, Brie, Roquefort, serve red Burgundy, Bordeaux, or Cabernet Sauvignon; with Swiss, a dry white (Neuchatel, Rhine, Riseling, Chablis, Moselle); with Gorgonzola, Romano, Bel Paese, red or white Chianti; with Stilton, port, cream sherry. General rule: Serve any dry red with full flavored cheese; any white with mild cheese.

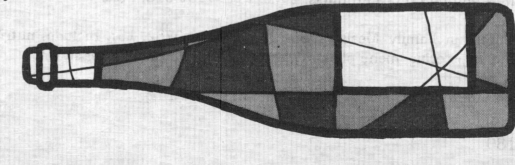

RECOMMENDATIONS

The following booklets are available from the government. Write to Consumer Product Information, Washington, D.C. 20407 for these booklets and/or a current catalogue of their offerings.

Family Food Buying: A guide for Calculating Amounts to Buy and Comparing Costs. 1969 60 pp. 0100-1117. 35¢

Some Questions and Answers About Food Additives. 1971. 4 pp. 7700-015. Free.

How to Buy Cheese. 1971. 24 pp. 0100-1441. 20¢

Milk and Milk-Type Products. 1970. 1 pg. 7700-018. Free.

Cheese in Family Meals. 1966. 22 pp. 0100-0782. 15¢. Includes nutritional importance, buying, storing, menu planning, and recipes with calories per serving.

Be sure to indicate catalogue number when ordering.

Index